Special Publication 800-144

I0002760

NIST

**National Institute of
Standards and Technology**

U.S. Department of Commerce

Guidelines on Security and Privacy in Public Cloud Computing

Wayne Jansen
Timothy Grance

NIST Special Publication 800-144

Guidelines on Security and Privacy in Public Cloud Computing

Wayne Jansen
Timothy Grance

C O M P U T E R   S E C U R I T Y

Computer Security Division
Information Technology Laboratory
National Institute of Standards and Technology
Gaithersburg, MD 20899-8930

December 2011

U.S. Department of Commerce

Rebecca M. Blank, Acting Secretary

National Institute of Standards and Technology

Patrick D. Gallagher, Under Secretary of Commerce for Standards and Technology and Director

Reports on Computer Systems Technology

The Information Technology Laboratory (ITL) at the National Institute of Standards and Technology (NIST) promotes the U.S. economy and public welfare by providing technical leadership for the Nation's measurement and standards infrastructure. ITL develops tests, test methods, reference data, proof of concept implementations, and technical analysis to advance the development and productive use of information technology. ITL's responsibilities include the development of technical, physical, administrative, and management standards and guidelines for the cost-effective security and privacy of sensitive unclassified information in Federal computer systems. This Special Publication discusses ITL's research, guidance, and outreach efforts in computer security, and its collaborative activities with industry, government, and academic organizations.

National Institute of Standards and Technology Special Publication 800-144
80 pages (December 2011)

Abstract

Cloud computing can and does mean different things to different people. The common characteristics most interpretations share are on-demand scalability of highly available and reliable pooled computing resources, secure access to metered services from nearly anywhere, and displacement of data and services from inside to outside the organization. While aspects of these characteristics have been realized to a certain extent, cloud computing remains a work in progress. This publication provides an overview of the security and privacy challenges pertinent to public cloud computing and points out considerations organizations should take when outsourcing data, applications, and infrastructure to a public cloud environment.

Keywords: *Cloud Computing; Computer Security and Privacy; Information Technology Outsourcing*

Acknowledgements

The authors, Wayne Jansen of Booz Allen Hamilton and Tim Grance of NIST, wish to thank colleagues who reviewed drafts of this document and contributed to its technical content, as well as the individuals who reviewed the public-release draft of this document and provided comments during the review period. In particular, Erika McCallister of NIST offered insight on the subject of privacy as it relates to cloud computing, and Tom Karygiannis and Ramaswamy Chandramouli, also from NIST, provided input on cloud security in early drafts. Thanks also go to Kevin Mills and Lee Badger, who assisted with our internal review process. Key improvements to this document would not have been possible without the feedback and valuable suggestions of all these individuals.

Table of Contents

Executive Summary

Cloud computing has been defined by NIST as a model for enabling convenient, on-demand network access to a shared pool of configurable computing resources (e.g., networks, servers, storage, applications, and services) that can be rapidly provisioned and released with minimal management effort or cloud provider interaction [Mel11]. Cloud computing technologies can be implemented in a wide variety of architectures, under different service and deployment models, and can coexist with other technologies and software design approaches. The security challenges cloud computing presents are formidable, including those faced by public clouds whose infrastructure and computational resources are owned and operated by an outside party that delivers services to the general public via a multi-tenant platform.

The emergence of cloud computing promises to have far-reaching effects on the systems and networks of federal agencies and other organizations. Many of the features that make cloud computing attractive, however, can also be at odds with traditional security models and controls. The primary purpose of this report is to provide an overview of public cloud computing and the security and privacy considerations involved. More specifically, this document describes the threats, technology risks, and safeguards surrounding public cloud environments, and their treatment. This document does not prescribe or recommend any specific cloud computing service, service arrangement, service agreement, service provider, or deployment model. Each organization is instead expected to apply the guidelines provided when performing its own analysis of its requirements, and to assess, select, engage, and oversee the public cloud services that can best fulfill those requirements.

The key guidelines from the report are summarized and listed below and are recommended to federal departments and agencies.

Carefully plan the security and privacy aspects of cloud computing solutions before engaging them.

Public cloud computing represents a significant paradigm shift from the conventional norms of an organizational data center to a deperimeterized infrastructure open to use by potential adversaries. As with any emerging information technology area, cloud computing should be approached carefully with due consideration to the sensitivity of data. Planning helps to ensure that the computing environment is as secure as possible and in compliance with all relevant organizational policies and that privacy is maintained. It also helps to ensure that the agency derives full benefit from information technology spending.

The security objectives of an organization are a key factor for decisions about outsourcing information technology services and, in particular, for decisions about transitioning organizational data, applications, and other resources to a public cloud computing environment. Organizations should take a risk-based approach in analyzing available security and privacy options and deciding about placing organizational functions into a cloud environment. The information technology governance practices of the organizations that pertain to the policies, procedures, and standards used for application development and service provisioning, as well as the design, implementation, testing, use, and monitoring of deployed or engaged services, should be extended to cloud computing environments.

To maximize effectiveness and minimize costs, security and privacy must be considered throughout the system lifecycle from the initial planning stage forward. Attempting to address security and privacy issues after implementation and deployment is not only much more difficult and expensive, but also exposes the organization to unnecessary risk.

Understand the public cloud computing environment offered by the cloud provider.

The responsibilities of both the organization and the cloud provider vary depending on the service model. Organizations consuming cloud services must understand the delineation of responsibilities over the computing environment and the implications for security and privacy. Assurances furnished by the cloud provider to support security or privacy claims, or by a certification and compliance review entity paid by the cloud provider, should be verified whenever possible through independent assessment by the organization.

Understanding the policies, procedures, and technical controls used by a cloud provider is a prerequisite to assessing the security and privacy risks involved. It is also important to comprehend the technologies used to provision services and the implications for security and privacy of the system. Details about the system architecture of a cloud can be analyzed and used to formulate a complete picture of the protection afforded by the security and privacy controls, which improves the ability of the organization to assess and manage risk accurately, including mitigating risk by employing appropriate techniques and procedures for the continuous monitoring of the security state of the system.

Ensure that a cloud computing solution satisfies organizational security and privacy requirements.

Public cloud providers' default offerings generally do not reflect a specific organization's security and privacy needs. From a risk perspective, determining the suitability of cloud services requires an understanding of the context in which the organization operates and the consequences from the plausible threats it faces. Adjustments to the cloud computing environment may be warranted to meet an organization's requirements. Organizations should require that any selected public cloud computing solution is configured, deployed, and managed to meet their security, privacy, and other requirements.

Non-negotiable service agreements in which the terms of service are prescribed completely by the cloud provider are generally the norm in public cloud computing. Negotiated service agreements are also possible. Similar to traditional information technology outsourcing contracts used by agencies, negotiated agreements can address an organization's concerns about security and privacy details, such as the vetting of employees, data ownership and exit rights, breach notification, isolation of tenant applications, data encryption and segregation, tracking and reporting service effectiveness, compliance with laws and regulations, and the use of validated products meeting federal or national standards (e.g., Federal Information Processing Standard 140). A negotiated agreement can also document the assurances the cloud provider must furnish to corroborate that organizational requirements are being met.

Critical data and applications may require an agency to undertake a negotiated service agreement in order to use a public cloud. Points of negotiation can negatively affect the economies of scale that a non-negotiable service agreement brings to public cloud computing, however, making a negotiated agreement less cost effective. As an alternative, the organization may be able to employ compensating controls to work around identified shortcomings in the public cloud service. Other alternatives include cloud computing environments with a more suitable deployment model, such as an internal private cloud, which can potentially offer an organization greater oversight and authority over security and privacy, and better limit the types of tenants that share platform resources, reducing exposure in the event of a failure or configuration error in a control.

With the growing number of cloud providers and range of services from which to choose, organizations must exercise due diligence when selecting and moving functions to the cloud. Decision making about services and service arrangements entails striking a balance between benefits in cost and productivity versus drawbacks in risk and liability. While the sensitivity of data handled by government organizations and the current state of the art make the likelihood of outsourcing all information technology services to a public cloud low, it should be possible for most government organizations to deploy some of their information technology services to a public cloud, provided that all requisite risk mitigations are taken.

Ensure that the client-side computing environment meets organizational security and privacy requirements for cloud computing.

Cloud computing encompasses both a server and a client side. With emphasis typically placed on the former, the latter can be easily overlooked. Services from different cloud providers, as well as cloud-based applications developed by the organization, can impose more exacting demands on the client, which may have implications for security and privacy that need to be taken into consideration.

Because of their ubiquity, Web browsers are a key element for client-side access to cloud computing services. Clients may also entail small lightweight applications that run on desktop and mobile devices to access services. The various available plug-ins and extensions for Web browsers are notorious for their security problems. Many browser add-ons also do not provide automatic updates, increasing the persistence of any existing vulnerabilities. Similar problems exist for other types of clients.

Maintaining physical and logical security over clients can be troublesome, especially with embedded mobile devices such as smart phones. Their size and portability can result in the loss of physical control. Built-in security mechanisms often go unused or can be overcome or circumvented without difficulty by a knowledgeable party to gain control over the device. Moreover, cloud applications are often delivered to them through custom-built native applications (i.e., apps) rather than a Web browser.

The growing availability and use of social media, personal Webmail, and other publicly available sites are a concern, since they increasingly serve as avenues for social engineering attacks that can negatively impact the security of the client, its underlying platform, and cloud services accessed. Having a backdoor Trojan, keystroke logger, or other type of malware running on a client device undermines the security and privacy of public cloud services as well as other Internet-facing public services accessed. As part of the overall cloud computing security architecture, organizations should review existing security and privacy measures and employ additional ones, if necessary, to secure the client side.

Maintain accountability over the privacy and security of data and applications implemented and deployed in public cloud computing environments.

Organizations should employ appropriate security management practices and controls over cloud computing. Strong management practices are essential for operating and maintaining a secure cloud computing solution. Security and privacy practices entail monitoring the organization's information system assets and assessing the implementation of policies, standards, procedures, controls, and guidelines that are used to establish and preserve the confidentiality, integrity, and availability of information system resources.

The organization should collect and analyze available data about the state of the system regularly and as often as needed to manage security and privacy risks, as appropriate for each level of the organization (i.e., governance level, mission or business process level, and information systems level) [Dem10]. Continuous monitoring of information security requires maintaining ongoing awareness of privacy and security controls, vulnerabilities, and threats to support risk management decisions. The goal is to conduct ongoing monitoring of the security of an organization's networks, information, and systems, and to respond by accepting, avoiding, or mitigating risk as situations change.

Assessing and managing risk in cloud computing systems can be a challenge, since significant portions of the computing environment are under the control of the cloud provider and may likely be beyond the organization's purview. Both qualitative and quantitative factors apply in a risk analysis. Risks must be carefully weighed against the available technical, management, and operational safeguards and the necessary steps must be taken to reduce risk to an acceptable level. The organization must also ensure that security and privacy controls are implemented correctly, operate as intended, and meet organizational requirements.

Establishing a level of confidence about a cloud service environment depends on the ability of the cloud provider to provision the security controls necessary to protect the organization's data and applications, and also the evidence provided about the effectiveness of those controls [JTF10]. Verifying the correct functioning of a subsystem and the effectiveness of security controls as extensively as with an internal organizational system may not be feasible in some cases, however, and other factors such as third-party audits may be used to establish a level of trust. Ultimately, if the level of confidence in the service falls below expectations and the organization is unable to employ compensating controls, it must either reject the service or accept a greater degree of risk.

Cloud computing depends on the security of many individual components. Besides components for general computing, there are also components that the management backplane comprises, such as those for self-service, resource metering, quota management, data replication and recovery, service level monitoring, and workload management. Many of the simplified interfaces and service abstractions afforded by cloud computing belie the inherent underlying complexity that affects security. Organizations should ensure to the maximum extent practicable that all cloud computing elements are secure and that security and privacy are maintained based on sound computing practices, including those outlined in Federal Information Processing Standards (FIPS) and NIST Special Publications (SP). The standards and guides listed in the table below provide material that is especially relevant to cloud computing and should be used in conjunction with this report.

Publication	Title
FIPS 199	Standards for Security Categorization of Federal Information and Information Systems
FIPS 200	Minimum Security Requirements for Federal Information and Information Systems
SP 800-18	Guide for Developing Security Plans for Federal Information Systems
SP 800-34, Revision 1	Contingency Planning Guide for Federal Information Systems
SP 800-37, Revision 1	Guide for Applying the Risk Management Framework to Federal Information Systems
SP 800-39	Managing Information Security Risk
SP 800-53, Revision 3	Recommended Security Controls for Federal Information Systems and Organizations
SP 800-53, Appendix J	Privacy Control Catalog
SP 800-53A, Revision 1	Guide for Assessing the Security Controls in Federal Information Systems
SP 800-60	Guide for Mapping Types of Information and Information Systems to Security Categories
SP 800-61, Revision 1	Computer Security Incident Handling Guide
SP 800-64, Revision 2	Security Considerations in the System Development Life Cycle
SP 800-86	Guide to Integrating Forensic Techniques into Incident Response
SP 800-88	Guidelines for Media Sanitization
SP 800-115	Technical Guide to Information Security Testing and Assessment
SP 800-122	Guide to Protecting the Confidentiality of Personally Identifiable Information (PII)
SP 800-137	Information Security Continuous Monitoring for Federal Information Systems and Organizations

1. Introduction

Interest in cloud computing has grown rapidly in recent years due to the advantages of greater flexibility and availability in obtaining computing resources at lower cost. Security and privacy, however, are a concern for agencies and organizations considering transitioning applications and data to public cloud computing environments, and form the impetus behind this document.

1.1 Authority

The National Institute of Standards and Technology (NIST) developed this document in furtherance of its statutory responsibilities under the Federal Information Security Management Act (FISMA) of 2002, Public Law 107-347.

NIST is responsible for developing standards and guidelines, including minimum requirements, for providing adequate information security for all agency operations and assets; but such standards and guidelines shall not apply to national security systems. This guideline is consistent with the requirements of the Office of Management and Budget (OMB) Circular A-130, Section 8b(3), "Securing Agency Information Systems," as analyzed in A-130, Appendix IV: Analysis of Key Sections. Supplemental information is provided in A-130, Appendix III.

This guideline has been prepared for use by federal agencies. It may be used by nongovernmental organizations on a voluntary basis and is not subject to copyright, though attribution is desired.

Nothing in this document should be taken to contradict standards and guidelines made mandatory and binding on federal agencies by the Secretary of Commerce under statutory authority, nor should these guidelines be interpreted as altering or superseding the existing authorities of the Secretary of Commerce, Director of the OMB, or any other federal official.

1.2 Purpose and Scope

The purpose of this document is to provide an overview of public cloud computing and the security and privacy challenges involved. The document discusses the threats, technology risks, and safeguards for public cloud environments, and provides the insight needed to make informed information technology decisions on their treatment. The document does not prescribe or recommend any specific cloud computing service, service arrangement, service agreement, service provider, or deployment model. Each organization must perform its own analysis of its needs, and assess, select, engage, and oversee the public cloud services that can best fulfill those needs.

1.3 Audience

The intended audience for this document includes the following categories of individuals:

- System managers, executives, and information officers making decisions about cloud computing initiatives

1

- Security professionals, including security officers, security administrators, auditors, and others with responsibility for information technology security

- Information technology program managers concerned with security and privacy measures for cloud computing

- System and network administrators

- Users of public cloud computing services.

This document, while technical in nature, provides background information to help readers understand the topics that are covered. The material presumes that readers possess fundamental operating system and networking expertise and have a basic understanding of cloud computing. Because of the evolving nature of security and privacy considerations in cloud computing, readers are expected to take advantage of other resources for more detailed and current information. These resources include the various publications listed or referenced in this document, the majority of which are available on-line.

1.4 Document Structure

The remainder of this document is organized into the following chapters:

- Chapter 2 presents an overview of public cloud computing.

- Chapter 3 discusses the benefits and drawbacks of public cloud services from a security and privacy perspective.

- Chapter 4 discusses key security and privacy issues in public cloud computing and precautions that can be taken to mitigate them.

- Chapter 5 provides guidance on addressing security and privacy issues when outsourcing support for data and applications to a cloud provider.

- Chapter 6 presents a short conclusion.

- Chapter 7 contains a list of references.

Sidebars containing auxiliary material related to the main discussion appear in gray text boxes throughout the main body of the document. At the end of the document, there are also appendices that contain supporting material: A list of acronyms is given in Appendix A, and a list of on-line resources can be found in Appendix B.

2. Background

Cloud computing has been defined by NIST as a model for enabling convenient, on-demand network access to a shared pool of configurable computing resources (e.g., networks, servers, storage, applications, and services) that can be rapidly provisioned and released with minimal management effort or cloud provider interaction [Mel11]. Cloud computing can be considered a new computing paradigm insofar as it allows the utilization of a computing infrastructure at one or more levels of abstraction, as an on-demand service made available over the Internet or other computer network. Because of the implications for greater flexibility and availability at lower cost, cloud computing is a subject that has been receiving a good deal of attention.

Cloud computing services benefit from economies of scale achieved through versatile use of resources, specialization, and other practicable efficiencies. However, cloud computing is an emerging form of distributed computing that is still undergoing evolution and standardization. The term itself is often used today with a range of meanings and interpretations [Fow09]. Much of what has been written about cloud computing is definitional, aimed at identifying important paradigms of deployment and use, and providing a general taxonomy for conceptualizing important facets of service.

2.1 Deployment Models

Public cloud computing is one of several deployment models that have been defined [Mel11]. Deployment models broadly characterize the management and disposition of computational resources for delivery of services to consumers, as well as the differentiation between classes of consumers. A public cloud is one in which the infrastructure and computational resources that it comprises are made available to the general public over the Internet. It is owned and operated by a cloud provider delivering cloud services to consumers and, by definition, is external to the consumers' organizations. At the other end of the spectrum are private clouds. A private cloud is one in which the computing environment is operated exclusively for a single organization. It may be managed by the organization or by a third party, and may be hosted within the organization's data center or outside of it. A private cloud has the potential to give the organization greater control over the infrastructure, computational resources, and cloud consumers than can a public cloud.

Two other deployment models exist: community and hybrid clouds. A community cloud falls between public and private clouds with respect to the target set of consumers. It is somewhat similar to a private cloud, but the infrastructure and computational resources are exclusive to two or more organizations that have common privacy, security, and regulatory considerations, rather than a single organization.[1] Hybrid clouds are more complex than the other deployment models, since they involve a composition of two or more clouds (private, community, or public). Each member remains a unique entity, but is bound to the others through standardized or proprietary technology that enables application and data portability among them.

---

[1] The term "organization" is used synonymously for "cloud consumer" throughout this publication.

While the choice of deployment model has implications for the security and privacy of a system, the deployment model itself does not dictate the level of security and privacy of specific cloud offerings. That level depends mainly on assurances, such as the soundness of the security and privacy policies, the robustness of the security and privacy controls, and the extent of visibility into performance and management details of the cloud environment, which are furnished by the cloud provider or independently attained by the organization (e.g., via independent vulnerability testing or auditing of operations).

2.2 Service Models

Just as deployment models play an important role in cloud computing, service models are also an important consideration. The service model to which a cloud conforms dictates an organization's scope and control over the computational environment, and characterizes a level of abstraction for its use. A service model can be actualized as a public cloud or as any of the other deployment models. Three well-known and often-used service models are the following [Lea09, Mel11, Vaq09, You08]:

- **Software-as-a-Service.** Software-as-a-Service (SaaS) is a model of service delivery whereby one or more applications and the computational resources to run them are provided for use on demand as a turnkey service. Its main purpose is to reduce the total cost of hardware and software development, maintenance, and operations. Security provisions are carried out mainly by the cloud provider. The cloud consumer does not manage or control the underlying cloud infrastructure or individual applications, except for preference selections and limited administrative application settings.

- **Platform-as-a-Service.** Platform-as-a-Service (PaaS) is a model of service delivery whereby the computing platform is provided as an on-demand service upon which applications can be developed and deployed. Its main purpose is to reduce the cost and complexity of buying, housing, and managing the underlying hardware and software components of the platform, including any needed program and database development tools. The development environment is typically special purpose, determined by the cloud provider and tailored to the design and architecture of its platform. The cloud consumer has control over applications and application environment settings of the platform. Security provisions are split between the cloud provider and the cloud consumer.

- **Infrastructure-as-a-Service.** Infrastructure-as-a-Service (IaaS) is a model of service delivery whereby the basic computing infrastructure of servers, software, and network equipment is provided as an on-demand service upon which a platform to develop and execute applications can be established. Its main purpose is to avoid purchasing, housing, and managing the basic hardware and software infrastructure components, and instead obtain those resources as virtualized objects controllable via a service interface. The cloud consumer generally has broad freedom to choose the operating system and development environment to be hosted. Security provisions beyond the basic infrastructure are carried out mainly by the cloud consumer.

4

Figure 1 illustrates the differences in scope and control between the cloud consumer and cloud provider for each of the service models discussed above. Five conceptual layers of a generalized cloud environment are identified in the center diagram and apply to public clouds, as well as each of the other deployment models. The arrows at the left and right of the diagram denote the approximate range of the cloud provider's and cloud consumer's scope and control over the cloud environment for each service model. In general, the higher the level of support available from a cloud provider, the more narrow the scope and control the cloud consumer has over the system.

The two lowest layers shown denote the physical elements of a cloud environment, which are under the full control of the cloud provider, regardless of the service model. Heating, ventilation, air conditioning (HVAC), power, communications, and other aspects of the physical plant form the bottom layer, the *facility layer*, while computers, network and storage components, and other physical computing infrastructure elements form the *hardware layer* immediately above it.

The remaining layers denote the logical elements of a cloud environment. The *virtualized infrastructure layer* entails software elements, such as hypervisors, virtual machines, virtual data storage, and virtual network components used to realize the infrastructure upon which a computing platform can be established. While virtual machine technology is commonly used at this layer, other means of providing the necessary software abstractions are not precluded. Similarly, the *platform architecture layer* entails compilers, libraries, utilities, middleware, and other software tools and development components needed to implement and deploy applications. The *application layer* represents deployed software applications that are targeted towards end-user software clients or other programs, and made available via the cloud.

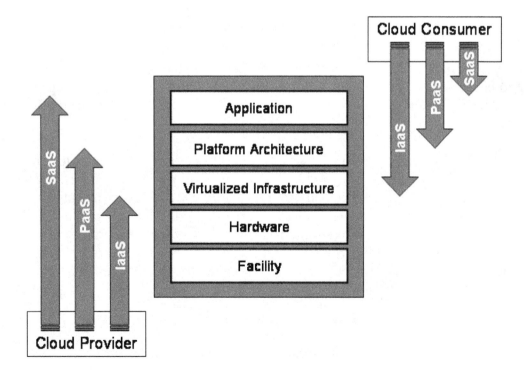

Figure 1: Differences in Scope and Control among Cloud Service Models

Some have argued that the distinction between IaaS and PaaS service models is fuzzy, and in many commercial offerings, the two are more alike than different [Arm10]. Nevertheless, these terms do serve a purpose, distinguishing between very basic support environments and environments having greater levels of support, and accordingly different allocations of control and responsibility between the cloud consumer and the cloud provider.

2.3 Outsourcing and Accountability

While cloud computing can be implemented exclusively for an organization as an internal private cloud, its main thrust has been to provide a vehicle for outsourcing parts of the organizational computing environment to an outside party via a public cloud. As with any outsourcing of information technology services, concerns exist about the implications for computer security and privacy. The main issue centers on the risks associated with moving important applications or data from within the confines of the organization's computing center to that of another organization (i.e., a public cloud), which is readily available for use by the general public.

Three broad classes of public clouds exist. The first class entails those with services that are provided at no cost to the consumer and are instead supported through advertisements. Search and electronic mail services are well-known examples. Such services may be limited to personal, non-commercial use. Information collected at registration and during use of the service may be combined with information obtained from other sources and used to deliver personalized advertisements to the consumer. Protection measures such as encrypted communications with the service may also be missing. The second class entails public clouds whose services are fee-based and free of advertisements. Services in this class can be similar to those of the first, but able to be offered at low cost to the consumer, because the terms of service delivery are non-negotiable and able to be modified unilaterally at the discretion of the cloud provider. Protection mechanisms that are beyond those of the first class and configurable by the consumer are typically provided. The third class entails public clouds whose services are fee-based and whose terms of service are negotiated between the organization and the cloud provider. While services are able to be tailored to the needs of the organization, the costs are generally dependent on the degree of deviation from the corresponding non-negotiable, fee-based services offered by the cloud provider.

Reducing cost and increasing efficiency are primary motivations for moving towards a public cloud, but relinquishing responsibility for security should not be. Ultimately, the organization is accountable for the choice of public cloud and the security and privacy of the outsourced service. Monitoring and addressing security issues that arise remain in the purview of the organization, as does oversight over other important issues such as performance and data privacy. Because cloud computing brings with it new security challenges, it is essential for an organization to oversee and manage how the cloud provider secures and maintains the computing environment and ensures data is kept secure.

3. Public Cloud Services

The outlook on cloud computing services can vary significantly among organizations, because of inherent differences in such things as the intended purpose, assets held, legal obligations, exposure to the public, threats faced, and tolerance to risk. For example, a government organization that predominantly handles data about individual citizens of the country has different privacy and security objectives from a government organization that does not. Similarly, the security objectives of a government organization that prepares and disseminates information for public consumption are different from one that deals mainly with classified information for its own internal use. From a risk perspective, determining the suitability of cloud services for an organization is not possible without understanding the context in which the organization operates and the consequences from the plausible threats it faces.

The set of security and privacy objectives of an organization, therefore, is a key factor for decisions about outsourcing information technology services and, in particular, for decisions about transitioning organizational resources to a public cloud and a specific provider's services and service arrangements. What works for one organization may not necessarily work for another. In addition, practical considerations apply—most organizations cannot afford financially to protect all computational resources and assets at the highest degree possible and must prioritize available options based on cost as well as criticality and sensitivity. When considering the potential benefits of public cloud computing, it is important to keep the organizational security and privacy objectives in mind and to act accordingly. Ultimately, a decision on cloud computing rests on a risk analysis of the tradeoffs involved.[2]

3.1 Service Agreements

Specifications for public cloud services and service arrangements are generally called service agreements or service contracts. A service agreement defines the terms and conditions for access and use of the services offered by the cloud provider. It also establishes the period of service, conditions for termination, and disposition of data (e.g., preservation period) upon termination. The complete terms and conditions for a cloud service agreement are usually stipulated in multiple documents, which can typically include a Service Level Agreement (SLA), privacy policy, acceptable use policy, and terms of use [Bra10]. An SLA represents the understanding between the cloud consumer and cloud provider about the expected level of service to be delivered and, in the event that the provider fails to deliver the service at the level specified, the compensation available to the cloud consumer. The privacy policy documents information handling practices and the way consumer information is collected, used, and managed by the cloud provider, while the acceptable use policy identifies prohibited behaviors by cloud consumers. The terms of use cover other important details such as licensing of services,

---

[2] The process to perform a risk analysis and manage risks is not discussed in this publication. For additional information, see NIST SP 800-30, *Risk Management Guide for Information Technology Systems*, and SP 800-37 Revision 1, *Guide for Applying the Risk Management Framework to Federal Information Systems*, at http://csrc.nist.gov/publications/PubsSPs.html.

limitations on liability, and modifications to the terms of the agreement. Privacy and security risks depend to a great extent on the terms established in the service agreement.

Two types of service agreements exist: predefined non-negotiable agreements and negotiated agreements [Bra10, UCG10]. Non-negotiable agreements are in many ways the basis for the economies of scale enjoyed by public cloud computing. The terms of service are prescribed completely by the cloud provider. They are typically not written with attention to federal privacy and security requirements [CIO10a]. Furthermore, with some offerings, the provider can make modifications to the terms of service unilaterally (e.g., by posting an updated version online) without giving any direct notification to the cloud consumer [Bra10].

Negotiated service agreements are more like traditional outsourcing contracts for information technology services. They can be used to address an organization's concerns about security and privacy policy, procedures, and technical controls, such as the vetting of employees, data ownership and exit rights, breach notification, isolation of tenant applications, data encryption and segregation, tracking and reporting service effectiveness, compliance with laws and regulations (e.g., Federal Information Security Management Act), and the use of validated products meeting national or international standards (e.g., Federal Information Processing Standard 140-2 for cryptographic modules).

Critical data and applications may require an agency to undertake a negotiated service agreement [Wal10]. Since points of negotiation can significantly perturb and negatively affect the economies of scale that a non-negotiable service agreement brings to public cloud computing, a negotiated service agreement is normally less cost effective. The outcome of a negotiation is also dependent on the size of the organization and the influence it can exert. Regardless of the type of service agreement, obtaining adequate legal and technical advice is recommended to ensure that the terms of service adequately meet the needs of the organization.

3.2 The Security and Privacy Upside

While one of the biggest obstacles facing public cloud computing is security, the cloud computing paradigm provides opportunities for innovation in provisioning security services that hold the prospect of improving the overall security of some organizations. The biggest beneficiaries are likely to be smaller organizations that have limited numbers of information technology administrators and security personnel, and can gain the economies of scale available to larger organizations with sizeable data centers, by transitioning to a public cloud.

Opportunities for improved security also benefit privacy. That is, effective privacy can exist only upon a sound foundation of information security. However, privacy, just as security, has broad organizational, operational, and technical implications. While some aspects of privacy are closely related to the confidentiality, integrity, and availability objectives of security, other aspects are not. Instead, they involve important privacy-related principles and considerations that are addressed in law, regulations, and OMB guidance [CIO10b].

Potential areas of improvement where organizations may derive security and privacy benefits from transitioning to a public cloud computing environment include the following:

- **Staff Specialization.** Cloud providers, just as other organizations with large-scale computing facilities, have an opportunity for staff to specialize in security, privacy, and other areas of high interest and concern to the organization. Increases in the scale of computing induce specialization, which in turn allows security staff to shed other duties and concentrate exclusively on security and privacy issues. Through increased specialization, there is an opportunity for staff members to gain in-depth experience and training, take remedial actions, and make improvements to security and privacy more readily than otherwise would be possible with a more diverse set of duties.

- **Platform Strength.** The structure of cloud computing platforms is typically more uniform than that of most traditional computing centers. Greater uniformity and homogeneity facilitate platform hardening and enable better automation of security management activities like configuration control, vulnerability testing, security audits, and security patching of platform components. Information assurance and security response activities also profit from a uniform, homogeneous cloud infrastructure, as do system management activities, such as fault management, load balancing, and system maintenance. Similarly, infrastructure homogeneity benefits management controls employed to protect privacy. On the other hand, homogeneity means that a single flaw will be manifested throughout the cloud, potentially impacting all tenants and services. Many cloud computing environments meet standards for operational compliance and certification in areas such as healthcare (e.g., Health Insurance Portability and Accountability Act (HIPAA)), finance (e.g., Payment Card Industry Data Security Standard (PCI DSS)), security (e.g., ISO 27001, Information Security Management Systems - Requirements), and audit (e.g., Standards for Attestation Engagements (SSAE) No. 16), and may attain formal certification or attestation from an independent third party, to impart a level of assurance with regard to some recognized and generally accepted criteria.

- **Resource Availability.** The scalability of cloud computing facilities allows for greater availability. Redundancy and disaster recovery capabilities are built into cloud computing environments and on-demand resource capacity can be used for better resilience when faced with increased service demands or distributed denial of service attacks, and for quicker recovery from serious incidents. When an incident occurs, an opportunity also exists to contain attacks and capture event information more readily, with greater detail and less impact on production. Availability can also bolster privacy through better opportunities for individuals to access and correct records and for records to be ready for use when needed for the purposes collected [CIO10b]. In some cases, however, such resiliency and capacity can have a downside. For example, an unsuccessful distributed denial of service attack can quickly consume large amounts of resources to defend against, which could inflict financial damage to an organization, if charges for increased usage in such situations are upheld. Access to vast amounts of inexpensive storage may also engender more information to be collected than needed or information to be retained longer than necessary.

- **Backup and Recovery.** The backup and recovery policies and procedures of a cloud provider may be superior to those of the organization and may be more robust. Data maintained within a cloud can be more available, faster to restore, and more reliable in many circumstances than that maintained in a traditional data center, and also meet offsite backup storage and geographical compliance requirements. Under such conditions, cloud services could also serve as an offsite repository for an organization's data center, in lieu of more traditional tape-based offsite storage [Kum08]. However, network performance over the Internet and the amount of data involved are limiting factors that can affect restoration.

- **Mobile Endpoints.** The architecture of a cloud solution extends to the client at the service endpoint that is used to access hosted applications. Cloud clients can be general-purpose Web browsers or more special-purpose applications. Since the main computational resources needed by cloud-based applications are typically held by the cloud provider, clients can generally be lightweight computationally and easily supported on laptops, notebooks, and netbooks, as well as embedded devices such as smart phones and tablets, benefiting the productivity of an increasingly mobile workforce.[3] One caveat to this point is that mobile devices, particularly embedded devices, require proper set up and protection to be of benefit overall, which include restrictions on the type of data maintained on the device [Jan08].

- **Data Concentration.** Data maintained and processed in a public cloud may present less of a risk to an organization with a mobile workforce than having that data dispersed on portable computers, embedded devices, or removable media out in the field, where theft and loss routinely occur. That is not to say, however, that no risk exists when data is concentrated.[4] Many organizations have made the transition to support access to organizational data from mobile devices to improve workflow management and gain other operational efficiencies and productivity benefits. Carefully constructed applications can restrict access and services to only the data and tasks that correspond strictly with the responsibilities a user needs to accomplish, limiting data exposure in the event of a device compromise.

3.3 The Security and Privacy Downside

Besides its many potential benefits for security and privacy, public cloud computing also brings with it potential areas of concern, when compared with computing environments found in traditional data centers. Some of the more fundamental concerns include the following:

- **System Complexity.** A public cloud computing environment is extremely complex compared with that of a traditional data center. Many components make up a public cloud, resulting in a large attack surface. Besides components for general computing, such as deployed applications, virtual machine monitors, guest virtual machines, data storage, and supporting middleware, there are also components that the management

---

[3] While not a security benefit per se, this item relates to the next bulleted item.

[4] See the next chapter for a discussion of the associated risks.

10

backplane comprises, such as those for self-service, resource metering, quota management, data replication and recovery, service level monitoring, workload management, and cloud bursting.[5] Cloud services themselves may also be realized through nesting and layering with services from other cloud providers. Components change over time as upgrades and feature improvements occur, confounding matters further.

Security depends not only on the correctness and effectiveness of many components, but also on the interactions among them. Challenges exist in understanding and securing application programming interfaces that are often proprietary to a cloud provider. The number of possible interactions between components increases as the square of the number of components, which pushes the level of complexity upward. Complexity typically relates inversely to security, with greater complexity giving rise to increased vulnerability [Avo00, Gee08, Sch00]. Decreases in security also heighten privacy risks related to the loss or unauthorized access, destruction, use, modification or disclosure of personal data.

- **Shared Multi-tenant Environment.** Public cloud services offered by providers have a serious underlying complication—client organizations typically share components and resources with other consumers that are unknown to them. Rather than using physical separation of resources as a control, cloud computing places greater dependence on logical separation at multiple layers of the application stack [Owa10]. While not unique to cloud computing, logical separation is a non-trivial problem that is exacerbated by the scale of cloud computing (e.g., [Bos11]). An attacker could pose as a consumer to exploit vulnerabilities from within the cloud environment, overcome the separation mechanisms, and gain unauthorized access. Access to organizational data and resources could also inadvertently be exposed to other consumers or be blocked from legitimate consumers through a configuration or software error [Opp03].

  Threats to network and computing infrastructures continue to increase each year and become more sophisticated. Having to share an infrastructure with unknown outside parties can be a major drawback for some applications and require a high level of assurance pertaining to the strength of the security mechanisms used for logical separation.

- **Internet-facing Services.** Public cloud services are delivered over the Internet, exposing the administrative interfaces used to self-service and manage an account, as well as non-administrative interfaces used to access deployed services.[6] Applications and data that

---

[5] Cloud bursting involves the deployment and launching of an application at a cloud and the redirection of requests to it, in the event that computing resources at organization's data center become saturated.

[6] Recommended solutions for mitigating Internet borne threats exist, including NIST Special publications SP 800-119, Guidelines for the Secure Deployment of IPv6--http://csrc.nist.gov/publications/nistpubs/800-119/sp800-119.pdf; SP 500-267, A Profile for IPv6 in the U.S. Government--Version 1.0--http://www.antd.nist.gov/usgv6/usgv6-v1.pdf; and SP-800-77, Guide to IPsec VPNs--http://csrc.nist.gov/publications/nistpubs/800-77/sp800-77.pdf. Support from the cloud provider is a prerequisite to implementing them, and as these publications correctly point out, exploits may still occur due to faulty implementation and configuration issues.

were previously accessed from the confines of an organization's intranet, but moved to a public cloud, must now face increased risk from network threats that were previously defended against at the perimeter of the organization's intranet and from new threats that target the exposed interfaces. The performance and quality of services delivered over the Internet may also be at issue. The effect is somewhat analogous to the inclusion of wireless access points into an organization's intranet at the onset of that technology, necessitating additional safeguards for secure use.

Relying on remote administrative access as the means for the organization to manage assets that are held within the cloud also increases risk, compared with a traditional data center, where administrative access to platforms can be restricted to direct or internal connections (e.g., [Som11]). Similarly, remote administrative access of the cloud infrastructure, if done by the cloud provider, is also a concern. When taken together with the previous two items, a highly complex, multi-tenanted computing environment, whose services are Internet-facing and available to the public, arguably affords a potentially attractive attack surface that must be carefully safeguarded.

- **Loss of Control.** While security and privacy concerns in cloud computing services are similar to those of traditional non-cloud services, they are amplified by external control over organizational assets and the potential for mismanagement of those assets. Transitioning to a public cloud requires a transfer of responsibility and control to the cloud provider over information as well as system components that were previously under the organization's direct control. The transition is usually accompanied by the lack of a direct point of contact with the management of operations and influence over decisions made about the computing environment. This situation makes the organization dependent on the cooperation of the cloud provider to carry out activities that span the responsibilities of both parties, such as continuous monitoring and incident response. Compliance with data protection laws and regulations is another important area of joint responsibility that requires coordination with and the cooperation of the cloud provider.

  Loss of control over both the physical and logical aspects of the system and data diminishes the organization's ability to maintain situational awareness, weigh alternatives, set priorities, and effect changes in security and privacy that are in the best interest of the organization. Legal protections for privacy may also be affected when information is stored with a third-party service provider [Cou09, Han06]. Under such conditions, maintaining accountability can be more challenging, offsetting some of the potential benefits discussed earlier.

A more detailed discussion of the security and privacy issues that stem from these fundamental concerns is given in the next chapter.

Other Kinds of Cloud Services. Other kinds of cloud services related to security and privacy exist. Besides providing a computing platform or substitute for in-house applications, public cloud services such as the following can also be focused on augmenting security in other computing environments:

- *Data Center Oriented.* Cloud services can be used to improve the security of data centers. Information about on-line activities collected from many participants from different organizations can allow for better threat monitoring. For example, electronic mail can be redirected to a cloud provider via mail exchange (MX) records, examined and analyzed collectively with similar transactions from other data centers to discover widespread spam, phishing, and malware campaigns, and to carry out remedial action (e.g., quarantining suspect messages and content) more comprehensively than a single organization would be able to do. Researchers have also successfully demonstrated a system architecture for provisioning cloud-based antivirus services, as an alternative to host-based antivirus solutions [Obe08b].

- *Cloud Oriented.* Cloud services can also be used to improve the security of other cloud environments. For example, reverse proxy products are available that enable unfettered access to a SaaS environment, yet maintain the data stored in that environment in encrypted form [Nav10]. Cloud-based identity management services also exist, which can be used to augment or replace an organization's directory service for identification and authentication of users to a cloud.

With any technology area, the functionality afforded can be turned towards improper or illicit activities. Cloud computing is no exception. A couple of noteworthy instances have already occurred that give a sense of what might be expected in the future:

- *Botnets.* In many ways, botnets assembled and controlled by hackers are an early form of cloud computing [Mul10]. Cost reduction, dynamic provisioning, redundancy, security, and many other characteristics of cloud computing apply. Botnets have been used for sending spam, harvesting login credentials, and launching injection attacks against Websites [Mul10, Pro09]. Botnets could be used to launch a denial of service attack against the infrastructure of a cloud provider. The possibility that a cloud service could become infiltrated by a botnet has already occurred; in 2009, a command-and-control node was discovered operating from within an IaaS cloud [Mcm09a, Whi09]. Spammers have also purchased cloud services directly to launch a phishing campaign, ensnaring recipients with malware via social engineering techniques [Cra08, Kre08].

- *Mechanism Cracking.* WiFi Protected Access (WPA) Cracker, a cloud service ostensibly for penetration testers, is an example of harnessing cloud resources on demand to break a cryptographic cipher and determine the encrypted password used to protect a wireless network. Through this service, a task that would take five days to run on a single computer can be accomplished in only 20 minutes on a cluster of 400 virtual machines [Rag09]. Because cryptography is used widely in authentication, data confidentiality and integrity, and other security mechanisms, these mechanisms become, in effect, less effective with the availability of cryptographic key cracking cloud services. Both cloud-based and traditional types of systems are possible targets. An IaaS cloud was reportedly used to attack an on-line gaming network and compromise the accounts of more than 100 million users [Alp11]. CAPTCHA cracking is another area where cloud services could be applied to bypass verification meant to thwart abusive use of Internet services by automated software.[7]

---

[7] CAPTCHA (Completely Automated Public Turing test to tell Computers and Humans Apart) involves the solution of a simple test by a user before gaining service, as a means of thwarting unwanted automated access.

4.   Key Security and Privacy Issues

Although the emergence of cloud computing is a recent development, insights into critical aspects of security can be gleaned from reported experiences of early adopters and also from researchers analyzing and experimenting with available cloud provider platforms and associated technologies. The sections below highlight privacy and security-related issues that are believed to have long-term significance for public cloud computing and, in many cases, for other cloud computing service models. Where possible, examples of previously exhibited or identified problems are provided to illustrate an issue. The examples are not exhaustive and may cover only one aspect of a more general issue. For many of the issues, the specific problems discussed have been resolved. Nevertheless, the broader issue persists in most cases and has the potential to be expressed again in other ways among the various service models. Security and privacy considerations that stem from information technology outsourcing also exist; they are covered in the next chapter and complement the material below.

Because cloud computing has grown out of an amalgamation of technologies, including service oriented architecture, virtualization, Web 2.0, and utility computing, many of the privacy and security issues involved can be viewed as known problems cast in a new setting. The importance of their combined effect in this setting, however, should not be discounted.   Public cloud computing does represent a thought-provoking paradigm shift from conventional norms to an open deperimeterized organizational infrastructure—*at the extreme, displacing applications from one organization's infrastructure to the infrastructure of another organization, where the applications of potential adversaries may also operate.*

4.1   Governance

Governance implies control and oversight by the organization over policies, procedures, and standards for application development and information technology service acquisition, as well as the design, implementation, testing, use, and monitoring of deployed or engaged services. With the wide availability of cloud computing services, lack of organizational controls over employees engaging such services arbitrarily can be a source of problems.   While cloud computing simplifies platform acquisition, it doesn't alleviate the need for governance; instead, it has the opposite effect, amplifying that need.

The ability to reduce capital investment for computing resources, and instead, satisfy computational needs through operational expenses is an advantage of cloud computing. Cloud computing can lower the initial cost of deploying new services and shorten the time required to gain a tangible benefit from the investment (i.e., accelerate the time-to-value), thus better aligning expense with actual use.[8]   However, the normal processes and procedures an organization uses to acquire computational resources as capital expenditures may be easily bypassed by a department or an individual, and the procuration obscured under day-to-day

---

[8] Many businesses also prefer operational expenses over capital expenditures, because of tax and other financial considerations (e.g., the ability to manage the cost of capital better and deduct operational expenses in the accounting period in which they are incurred versus depreciating the capital expenditure over time).

operational expenses.[9] If such actions are not governed by an organization, its policies and procedures for privacy, security, and oversight could be overlooked and the organization put at risk. For example, vulnerable systems could be deployed, legal regulations could be ignored, charges could amass quickly to unacceptable levels, resources could be used for unsanctioned purposes, or other untoward effects could occur.

A study involving more than nine hundred information technology professionals in Europe and the United States indicates a strong concern by participants that cloud computing services may have been deployed without their knowledge in parts of their respective organizations [Pon10]. The issue is somewhat akin to the problem with individuals setting up rogue wireless access points tied into the organizational infrastructure—without proper governance, the organizational computing infrastructure could be transformed into a sprawling, unmanageable mix of insecure services. Organizational practices pertaining to the policies, procedures, and standards used for application development and service acquisition, as well as the design, implementation, testing, use, and monitoring of deployed or engaged services, should be extended to cover cloud computing environments.

Dealing with cloud services requires attention to the roles and responsibilities involved between the organization and cloud provider, particularly with respect to managing risks and ensuring organizational requirements are met. Ensuring systems are secure and risk is managed is challenging in any environment and even more daunting with cloud computing. Audit mechanisms and tools should be in place to determine how data is stored, protected, and used, to validate services, and to verify policy enforcement. A risk management program should also be in place that is flexible enough to deal with the continuously evolving and shifting risk landscape.

4.2 Compliance

Compliance refers to an organization's responsibility to operate in agreement with established laws, regulations, standards, and specifications. Various types of security and privacy laws and regulations exist within different countries at the national, state, and local levels, making compliance a potentially complicated issue for cloud computing. For example, at the end of 2010, the National Conference of State Legislatures reported that forty-six states have enacted legislation governing disclosure of security breaches of personal information, and that at least twenty-nine states have enacted laws governing the disposal of personal data held by businesses and/or government.[10]

- **Law and Regulations.** For U.S. Federal agencies, the major security and privacy compliance concerns include the Clinger-Cohen Act of 1996, the Office of Management and Budget (OMB) Circular No. A-130, particularly Appendix III, the Privacy Act of

---

[9] Combating improper and abusive purchases in the federal government demands constant vigilance. For example, see the U.S. Government Accountability Office's report on Government-wide Purchase Cards: Actions Needed to Strengthen Internal Controls to Reduce Fraudulent, Improper, and Abusive Purchases at http://www.gao.gov/new.items/d08333.pdf.

[10] For more detailed information, see Issues & Research on Telecommunications & Information Technology at http://www.ncsl.org/.

15

1974, the E-Government Act of 2002 and its accompanying OMB guidance, and the Federal Information Security Management Act (FISMA) of 2002.[11] Also of importance are National Archives and Records Administration (NARA) statutes, including the Federal Records Act (44 U.S.C. Chapters 21, 29, 31, 33) and NARA regulations (Title 36 of the Code of Federal Regulations, Chapter XII, Subchapter B).

The Clinger-Cohen Act assigns responsibilities for the efficiency, security, and privacy of computer systems within the federal government and establishes a comprehensive approach for executive agencies to improve the acquisition and management of their information resources. As part of OMB's responsibilities under the Clinger-Cohen act, various circulars have been issued. Circular A-130 establishes policy for the management of Federal information resources, including procedural and analytic guidelines for implementing specific aspects of these policies. Appendix III of A-130 requires that adequate security is provided for all agency information that is collected, processed, transmitted, stored, or disseminated in general support systems and major applications.

The Privacy Act governs the collection, maintenance, use, and dissemination of information about individuals that is maintained in systems of records by federal agencies and can be retrieved by a personal identifier (e.g., name). It requires each agency to publish notice of its systems of records (i.e., a system of records notice (SORN)) in the Federal Register and to allow individuals to request access to and correction of their records and information. The E-Government Act of 2002, among other things, requires federal agencies to complete a Privacy Impact Assessment (PIA) on all new or substantially changed technology that collects, maintains, or disseminates PII, and to make the results publicly available. M-03-22, OMB Guidance for Implementing the Privacy Provisions of the E-Government Act of 2002, provides direction to agencies on conducting PIAs. A PIA is a structured review of an information system to identify and mitigate privacy risks, including risks to confidentiality, at every stage of the system lifecycle. It can also serve as a tool for individuals working on a program or accessing a system to understand how to best integrate privacy protections when working with PII.

FISMA requires federal agencies to adequately protect their information and information systems against unauthorized access, use, disclosure, disruption, modification, or destruction [HR2458]. That mandate includes protecting information systems used or operated by an agency or by a contractor of an agency or other organization on behalf of an agency. That is, any external provider handling federal information or operating information systems on behalf of the federal government must meet the same security requirements as the source federal agency. The security requirements also apply to external subsystems storing, processing, or transmitting federal information and any services provided by, or associated with, the subsystem.

---

[11] FISMA is Title III of the E-Government Act of 2002, Public Law No. 107-347.

Under the Federal Records Act and NARA regulations, agencies are responsible for managing federal records effectively throughout their lifecycle, including records in electronic information systems and in contracted environments. If a contractor holds federal records, the contractor must manage them in accordance with all applicable records management laws and regulations. Managing the records includes secure storage, retrievability, and proper disposition, including transfer of permanently valuable records to NARA in an acceptable format [Fer10].

Other government and industry-association requirements, such as the Health Insurance Portability and Accountability Act (HIPAA) and the Payment Card Industry Data Security Standard (PCI DSS), may apply to a particular organization. For example, the Veterans Health Administration falls under HIPAA regulations for private and public health care facilities, which apply to both employees and contractors [DVA]. HIPAA requires both technical and physical safeguards for controlling access to protected health information, which may create compliance issues for some cloud providers.

Cloud providers are becoming more sensitive to legal and regulatory concerns, and may be willing to commit to store and process data in specific jurisdictions and apply required safeguards for security and privacy. However, the degree to which they will accept liability in their service agreements, for exposure of content under their control, remains to be seen. Even so, organizations are ultimately accountable for the security and privacy of data held by a cloud provider on their behalf.

- **Data Location.** One of the most common compliance issues facing an organization is data location [Bin09, Kan09, Ove10]. Use of an in-house computing center allows an organization to structure its computing environment and to know in detail where data is stored and what safeguards are used to protect the data. In contrast, a characteristic of many cloud computing services is that data is stored redundantly in multiple physical locations and detailed information about the location of an organization's data is unavailable or not disclosed to the service consumer. This situation makes it difficult to ascertain whether sufficient safeguards are in place and whether legal and regulatory compliance requirements are being met. For example, NARA regulations (i.e., 36 CFR 1234) include facility requirements for the storage of federal records and stipulate a minimum height above and distance away from a flood plain. External audits and security certifications can alleviate this issue to some extent, but they are not a panacea [Mag10].

When information crosses borders, the governing legal, privacy, and regulatory regimes can be ambiguous and raise a variety of concerns (e.g., [CBC04, Wei11]). Consequently, constraints on the transborder flow of sensitive data, as well as the requirements on the protection afforded the data, have become the subject of national and regional privacy and security laws and regulations [Eis05].

The main compliance concerns with transborder data flows include whether the laws in the jurisdiction where the data was collected permit the flow, whether those laws continue to apply to the data post transfer, and whether the laws at the destination present additional risks or benefits [Eis05]. Technical, physical and administrative safeguards, such as access controls, often apply. For example, European data protection laws may impose additional obligations on the handling and processing of data transferred to the U.S. [DoC00]. These concerns can be alleviated if the cloud provider has some reliable means to ensure that an organization's data is stored and processed only within specific jurisdictions.

- **Electronic Discovery.** Electronic discovery involves the identification, collection, processing, analysis, and production of Electronically Stored Information (ESI) in the discovery phase of litigation [Daw05]. Organizations also have other incentives and obligations to preserve and produce electronic documents, such as complying with audit and regulatory information requests, and for government organizations, complying with Freedom of Information Act (FOIA) requests. ESI includes not only electronic mail, attachments, and other data objects stored on a computer system or storage media, but also any associated metadata, such as dates of object creation or modification, and non-rendered file content (i.e., data that is not explicitly displayed for consumers).

  The capabilities and processes of a cloud provider, such as the form in which data is maintained and the electronic discovery-related tools available, affect the ability of the organization to meet its obligations in a cost effective, timely, and compliant manner [Mcd10]. For example, a cloud provider's archival capabilities may not preserve the original metadata as expected, causing spoliation (i.e., the intentional, reckless, or negligent destruction, loss, material alteration, or obstruction of evidence that is relevant to litigation), which could negatively impact litigation. The cloud provider's electronic discovery capabilities and processes must not compromise the privacy or security of the data and applications of the organization in satisfying the discovery obligations of other cloud consumers, and vice versa.

4.3 Trust

Under the cloud computing paradigm, an organization relinquishes direct control over many aspects of security and privacy, and in doing so, confers a high level of trust onto the cloud provider. At the same time, federal agencies have a responsibility to protect information and information systems commensurate with the risk and magnitude of the harm resulting from unauthorized access, use, disclosure, disruption, modification, or destruction, regardless of whether the information is collected or maintained by or on behalf of the agency; or whether the information systems are used or operated by an agency or by a contractor of an agency or other organization on behalf of an agency [HR2458].

- **Insider Access.** Data processed or stored outside the physical confines of an organization, its firewall, and other security controls bring with it an inherent level of risk. The insider security threat is a well-known issue for most organizations and, despite the name, applies as well to outsourced cloud services [Ash10, Cap09, Kow08]. Insider threats go beyond those posed by current or former employees to include contractors, organizational affiliates, and other parties that have received access to an organization's networks, systems, and data to carry out or facilitate operations. Incidents may involve various types of fraud, sabotage of information resources, and theft of sensitive information. Incidents may also be caused unintentionally—for instance, a bank employee reportedly sent out sensitive customer information to the wrong Google mail account [Zet09b].

Moving data and applications to a cloud computing environment operated by a cloud provider expands the circle of insiders not only to the cloud provider's staff and subcontractors, but also potentially to other customers using the service, thereby increasing risk. For example, a denial of service attack launched by a malicious insider was demonstrated against a well-known IaaS cloud [Mee09, Sla09]. The attack involved a cloud consumer creating an initial 20 accounts and launching virtual machine instances for each, then using those accounts to create an additional 20 accounts and machine instances in an iterative fashion, exponentially growing and consuming resources beyond set limits.

- **Data Ownership.** The organization's ownership rights over the data must be firmly established in the service contract to enable a basis for trust and privacy of data. The continuing controversy over privacy and data ownership rights for social networking users illustrates the impact that ambiguous terms can have on the parties involved (e.g., [Goo10, Rap09]). Ideally, the contract should state clearly that the organization retains exclusive ownership over all its data; that the cloud provider acquires no rights or licenses through the agreement, including intellectual property rights or licenses, to use the organization's data for its own purposes; and that the cloud provider does not acquire and may not claim any interest in the data due to security [Mcd10]. For these provisions to work as intended, the terms of data ownership must not be subject to unilateral amendment by the cloud provider.

- **Composite Services.** Cloud services themselves can be composed through nesting and layering with other cloud services. For example, a public SaaS provider could build its services upon those of a PaaS or IaaS cloud. The level of availability of the SaaS cloud would then depend on the availability of those services. If the percent availability of a support service drops, the overall availability suffers proportionally.

Cloud services that use third-party cloud providers to outsource or subcontract some of their services should raise concerns, including the scope of control over the third party, the responsibilities involved (e.g., policy and licensing arrangements), and the remedies and recourse available should problems occur. Public cloud providers that host applications or services of other parties may involve other domains of control, but through transparent authentication mechanisms, appear to a consumer to be that of the cloud provider. Trust is often not transitive, requiring that third-party arrangements are disclosed in advance of reaching an agreement with the cloud provider, and that the terms of these arrangements are maintained throughout the agreement or until sufficient notification can be given of any anticipated changes.

Liability and performance guarantees can become a serious issue with composite cloud services. For example, a consumer storage-based social networking service closed down after losing access to a significant amount of data from 20,000 of its clients. Because it relied on another cloud provider to host historical data, and on yet another cloud provider to host its newly launched application and database, direct responsibility for the cause of the failure was unclear and never resolved [Bro08].

■ **Visibility.** Continuous monitoring of information security requires maintaining ongoing awareness of security controls, vulnerabilities, and threats to support risk management decisions [Dem10]. Collecting and analyzing available data about the state of the system should be done regularly and as often as needed by the organization to manage security and privacy risks, as appropriate for each level of the organization involved in decision making. Transition to public cloud services entails a transfer of responsibility to the cloud provider for securing portions of the system on which the organization's data and applications operate. To fulfill the obligations of continuous monitoring, the organization is dependent on the cloud provider, whose cooperation is essential, since aspects of the computing environment are under the cloud provider's complete control.

Knowledge of a cloud provider's security measures is also needed for the organization to conduct risk management. For example, the process of identifying vulnerabilities should include an analysis of the system security features and the security controls used to protect the cloud environment [Sto02]. Cloud providers can be reluctant to provide details of their security and privacy measures and status, however, since such information is often considered proprietary and might otherwise be used to devise an avenue of attack. Moreover, detailed network and system level monitoring by a cloud consumer is generally not part of most service arrangements, limiting visibility and the means to audit operations directly (e.g., [Bro09, Dig08, Met09]). While notification tools and Web-based dashboards are typically made available to consumers to monitor status, they can lack sufficient detail and may themselves suffer disruption during a system outage [Goo09a, Ker11, Per11].

Transparency in the way the cloud provider operates, including the provisioning of composite services, is a vital ingredient for effective oversight over system security and privacy by an organization. To ensure that policy and procedures are being enforced throughout the system lifecycle, service arrangements should include some means for the organization to gain visibility into the security controls and processes employed by the cloud provider and their performance over time. For example, the service agreement could include the right to audit controls via a third party, as a way to validate control aspects that are not otherwise accessible or assessable by the consumer. Ideally, the consumer would have control over aspects of the means of visibility to accommodate its needs, such as the threshold for alerts and notifications, and the level of detail and schedule of reports.

■ **Ancillary Data.** While the focus of attention in cloud computing is mainly on protecting application data, cloud providers also hold significant details about the accounts of cloud consumers that could be compromised and used in subsequent attacks. Payment information is one example; other, more subtle types of information, can also be involved. For example, a database of contact information stolen from a SaaS cloud provider, via a targeted phishing attack against one of its employees, was used in turn to

20

launch successful targeted electronic mail attacks against consumers of the cloud service [Kre07, Mcm07]. The incident illustrates the need for cloud providers to protect and report promptly security breaches occurring not only in the data the cloud provider holds for its consumers, but also in the data it holds *about* its consumers, regardless of whether the data is held within or separately from the cloud infrastructure.

Other types of ancillary data that exists involve information the cloud provider collects or produces about customer-related activity in the cloud. They include data collected to meter and charge for consumption of resources, logs and audit trails, and other such metadata that is generated and accumulated within the cloud environment. Unlike organizational data, a cloud provider may be more inclined to claim ownership over the operational and other types of metadata it collects. Such data, if sold, released, or leaked to a third party, however, is a potential threat to an organization's privacy, since the data could be used to infer the status and outlook of an organization's initiative (e.g., the activity level or projected growth of a startup company). Several points to consider clarifying in a service contract are the types of metadata collected by the cloud provider, the protection afforded the metadata, and the organization's rights over metadata, including ownership, opting out of collection or distribution, and fair use.

■ **Risk Management.** With cloud-based services, some subsystems or subsystem components fall outside of the direct control of a client organization. Many organizations are more comfortable with risk when they have greater control over the processes and equipment involved. At a minimum, a high degree of control provides the option to weigh alternatives, set priorities, and act decisively in the best interest of the organization when faced with an incident. Risk management is the process of identifying and assessing risk to organizational operations, organizational assets, or individuals resulting from the operation of an information system, and taking the necessary steps to reduce it to an acceptable level [Sto02]. The process includes the conduct of a risk assessment, the implementation of a risk mitigation strategy, and the employment of techniques and procedures for the continuous monitoring of the security state of the information system.[12] Public cloud-based systems, as with traditional information systems, require that risks are managed throughout the system lifecycle.

Assessing and managing risk in systems that use cloud services can be a challenge. FISMA and OMB policy require external providers handling federal information or operating information systems on behalf of the federal government to meet the same security requirements as federal agencies [JTF10]. To the maximum extent practicable, organizations should ensure that privacy and security controls are implemented correctly, operate as intended, and meet its requirements. Organizations should understand the privacy and security controls of the cloud service, establish adequate arrangements in the

---

[12] For more detailed information about risk management, see NIST SP 800-37 Revision 1, *Guide for Applying the Risk Management Framework to Federal Information Systems*– http://csrc.nist.gov/groups/SMA/fisma/framework.html.

service agreement, making any needed adjustments, and monitor compliance of the service controls with the terms of the agreement.

Establishing a level of trust about a cloud service is dependent on the degree of control an organization is able to exert on the provider to provision the security controls necessary to protect the organization's data and applications, and also the evidence provided about the effectiveness of those controls [JTF10]. However, verifying the correct functioning of a subsystem and the effectiveness of security controls as extensively as with an organizational system may not be feasible in some cases, and other means (e.g., third-party audits) may be used to establish a level of trust. Ultimately, if the level of trust in the service falls below expectations and the organization is unable to employ compensating controls, it must either reject the service or accept a greater degree of risk.

4.4 Architecture

The architecture of the software and hardware used to deliver cloud services can vary significantly among public cloud providers for any specific service model. The physical location of the infrastructure is determined by the cloud provider as is the design and implementation of the reliability, resource pooling, scalability, and other logic needed in the support framework. Applications are built on the programming interfaces of Internet-accessible services, which typically involve multiple cloud components communicating with each other over application programming interfaces. Virtual machines typically serve as the abstract unit of deployment for IaaS clouds and are loosely coupled with the cloud storage architecture. Cloud providers may also use other computing abstractions in lieu of virtual machine technology to provision services for other service models.

To complement the server side of the equation, cloud-based applications require a client side to initiate and obtain services. While Web browsers often serve as clients, other possibilities exist. In addition, an adequate and secure network communications infrastructure must be in place. Many of the simplified interfaces and service abstractions on the client, server, and network belie the inherent underlying complexity that affects security and privacy. Therefore, it is important to understand the technologies the cloud provider uses to provision services and the implications the technical controls involved have on security and privacy of the system throughout its lifecycle. With such information, the underlying system architecture of a cloud can be decomposed and mapped to a framework of security and privacy controls that can be used to assess and manage risk.

- **Attack Surface.** The hypervisor or virtual machine monitor is an additional layer of software between an operating system and hardware platform that is used to operate multi-tenant virtual machines and is common to IaaS clouds. Besides virtualized resources, the hypervisor normally supports other application programming interfaces to conduct administrative operations, such as launching, migrating, and terminating virtual machine instances. Compared with a traditional, non-virtualized implementation, the addition of a hypervisor causes an increase in the attack surface. That is, there are additional methods (e.g., application programming interfaces), channels (e.g., sockets), and data items (e.g., input strings) an attacker can use to cause damage to the system.

22

The complexity in virtual machine environments can also be more challenging than in their traditional counterparts, giving rise to conditions that undermine security [Gar05]. For example, paging, checkpointing, and migration of virtual machines can leak sensitive data to persistent storage, subverting protection mechanisms in the hosted operating system intended to prevent such occurrences. Moreover, the hypervisor itself can potentially be compromised. A compromise of the hypervisor could result in the compromise of all systems that it hosts [Sca11]. For instance, a vulnerability that allowed specially crafted File Transfer Protocol (FTP) requests to corrupt a heap buffer in the hypervisor, which in turn could induce the execution of arbitrary code at the host, was discovered in the Network Address Translation (NAT) routine of a widely used virtualization software product [Sec05, She05].

Virtual servers and applications, much like their non-virtual counterparts, need to be secured, both physically and logically. Following organizational policies and procedures, the operating system and applications should be hardened when producing virtual machine images for deployment. Care must also be taken to provision security for the virtualized environments in which the images run [You07]. For example, virtual firewalls can be used to isolate groups of virtual machines from other hosted groups, such as production systems from development systems or development systems from other cloud-resident systems. Carefully managing virtual machine images is also important to avoid accidentally deploying images under development or containing vulnerabilities.

■ **Virtual Network Protection.** Most virtualization platforms have the ability to create software-based switches and network configurations as part of the virtual environment to allow virtual machines on the same host to communicate more directly and efficiently. For example, for virtual machines requiring no external network access, the virtual networking architectures of most virtualization software products support same-host networking, in which a private subnet is created for intra-host communications. Traffic over virtual networks may not be visible to security protection devices on the physical network, such as network-based intrusion detection and prevention systems [Sca11, Vie09]. To avoid a loss of visibility and protection against intra-host attacks, duplication of the physical network protection capabilities may be required on the virtual network [Ref10, Vmw10]. While some hypervisors allow network monitoring, their capabilities are generally not as robust as those in tools used to monitor physical networks. Organizations should consider the risk and performance tradeoffs between having traffic hidden within the hypervisor versus exposing that traffic to the physical network for monitoring [Sca11].

A side effect of virtualized environments is the potential loss of separation of duties between existing administration roles in an organization. For example, in traditional computing environments, computer administrators typically do not configure network security components, such as intrusion detection and prevention systems and firewalls. Network security administrators, on the other hand, can configure such devices, but typically do not have administrative rights on hosts to grant system access. In virtual environments, the distinct roles of computer and network security administrators can collapse into a single role of a virtual infrastructure administrator. Other distinct roles,

23

such as that of storage administrators, can be similarly affected. Management and operational controls may be needed to compensate a lack of technical controls in virtual environments for maintaining separation of duty.

Virtual Machine Images. IaaS cloud providers and manufacturers of virtual machine products maintain repositories of virtual machine images. A virtual machine image entails the software stack, including installed and configured applications, used to boot the virtual machine into an initial state or the state of some previous checkpoint. Sharing virtual machine images is a common practice in some cloud computing environments as a quick way to get started. Virtual machine images created by the organization must be carefully managed and controlled to avoid problems. For instance, images need to be kept up-to-date with the latest security patches. Caution must be taken to avoid using images that have not been vetted or releasing images in a haphazard fashion.

The provider of an image faces risks, since an image can contain proprietary code and data and embody vulnerabilities. An attacker may attempt to examine images to determine whether they leak information or provide an avenue for attack [Wei09]. This is especially true of development images that are accidentally released. The reverse may also occur—an attacker may attempt to supply a virtual machine image containing malware to consumers of a cloud computing system [Jen09, Wei09].[13] For example, researchers demonstrated that by manipulating the registration process to gain a first-page listing, they could readily entice cloud consumers to run virtual machine images they contributed to the image repository of a popular cloud provider [Mee09, Sla09]. The risks for consumers running tainted images include theft and corruption of data. Organizations should consider implementing a formal image management process to govern the creation, storage, and use of virtual machine images [Sca11].

■ **Client-Side Protection.** A successful defense against attacks requires securing both the client and server side of cloud computing. With emphasis typically placed on the latter, the former can be easily overlooked. Services from different cloud providers, as well as cloud-based applications developed by the organization, can impose more exacting demands on the client, which may have implications for security and privacy that need to be taken into consideration. Web browsers, a key element for many cloud computing services, and the various plug-ins and extensions available for them are notorious for their security problems [Jen09, Ker10, Pro07, Pro09]. Moreover, many browser add-ons do not provide automatic updates, increasing the persistence of any existing vulnerabilities.

Maintaining physical and logical security over clients can be troublesome, especially with embedded mobile devices such as smart phones. Their size and portability can result in the loss of physical control. Built-in security mechanisms often go unused or can be overcome or circumvented without difficulty by a knowledgeable party to gain control

---

[13] For PaaS and SaaS environments, a malicious implementation module is supplied.

24

over the device [Jan08]. Smart phones are also treated more as fixed appliances with a limited set of functions, than as general-purpose systems. Moreover, cloud applications are often delivered to them through custom-built native applications (i.e., apps) rather than a Web browser. No single operating system dominates smart phones, and security patches and updates for system components are not as frequent as for desktop computers, making vulnerabilities more persistent and widening the window of opportunity for exploitation. As a safeguard, organizations can prohibit or strictly limit access to PII and other sensitive data from portable and mobile devices and reduce risk [Mcc10].

The growing availability and use of social media, personal Webmail, and other publicly available sites also have associated risks that are a concern, since they increasingly serve as avenues for social engineering attacks that can negatively impact the security of the browser, its underlying platform, and cloud services accessed. For example, spyware was reportedly installed in a hospital system via an employee's personal Webmail account and sent the attacker more than 1,000 screen captures, containing financial and other confidential information, before being discovered [Mcm09b]. Having a backdoor Trojan, keystroke logger, or other type of malware present on a client, runs counter to protecting the security and privacy of public cloud services, as well as other Internet-facing public services being accessed [Fre08, MRG10].

As part of the overall security architecture for cloud computing, organizations need to review existing measures and employ additional ones, if necessary, to secure the client side. Banks are beginning to take the lead in deploying hardened browser environments that encrypt network exchanges and protect against keystroke logging [Dun10a, Dun10b]. Security awareness training also is an important measure for an organization to apply, since the proper behavior of individuals is an essential safeguard against many types of attacks.

4.5 Identity and Access Management

Data sensitivity and privacy of information have become increasingly an area of concern for organizations. The identity proofing and authentication aspects of identity management entail the use, maintenance, and protection of PII collected from users. Preventing unauthorized access to information resources in the cloud is also a major consideration. One recurring issue is that the organizational identification and authentication framework may not naturally extend into a public cloud and extending or changing the existing framework to support cloud services may prove difficult [Cho09]. The alternative of employing two different authentication systems, one for the internal organizational systems and another for external cloud-based systems, is a complication that can become unworkable over time. Identity federation, popularized with the introduction of service oriented architectures, is one solution.

Identity federation allows the organization and cloud provider to trust and share digital identities and attributes across both domains, and to provide a means for single sign-on. For federation to succeed, identity and access management transactions must be interpreted carefully and unambiguously and protected against attacks. Clear separation of the managed identities of the cloud consumer from those of the cloud provider must also be ensured to protect the consumer's resources from provider-authenticated entities and vice versa. Identity federation can be accomplished in a number of ways, such as with the Security Assertion Markup Language (SAML) standard or the OpenID standard.

- **Authentication.** Authentication is the process of establishing confidence in user identities. Authentication assurance levels should be appropriate for the sensitivity of the application and information assets accessed and the risk involved [Bur06]. A growing number of cloud providers support the SAML standard and use it to administer users and authenticate them before providing access to applications and data. SAML provides a means to exchange information between cooperating domains. For example, a SAML transaction can convey assertions that a user has been authenticated by an identity provider and also include information about the user's privileges. Upon receipt of the transaction, the service provider then uses the information to grant the user an appropriate level of access, once the identity and credentials supplied for the user are successfully verified.

  SAML request and response messages are typically mapped over SOAP,[14] which relies on the eXtensible Markup Language (XML) for its format. SOAP messages are digitally signed. In a public cloud, for instance, once a user has established a public key certificate with the service, the private key can be used to sign SOAP requests.

  SOAP message security validation is complicated and must be carried out carefully to prevent attacks. XML wrapping attacks have been successfully demonstrated against a public IaaS cloud [Gru09]. XML wrapping involves manipulation of SOAP messages. A new element (i.e., the wrapper) is introduced into the SOAP Security header; the original message body is then moved under the wrapper and replaced by a bogus body containing an operation defined by the attacker [Gaj09, Gru09]. The original body can still be referenced and its signature verified, but the operation in the replacement body is executed instead.

- **Access Control.** SAML alone is not sufficient to provide cloud-based identity and access management services. The capability to adapt cloud consumer privileges and maintain control over access to resources is also needed. As part of identity management, standards like the eXtensible Access Control Markup Language (XACML) can be used by a cloud provider to control access to cloud resources, in lieu of some proprietary means. The XACML standard defines an XML-based language for stating policy and forming access control decisions. XACML focuses on the mechanism for arriving at authorization decisions, which complements SAML's focus on the means for transferring authentication and authorization decisions between cooperating entities.

  XACML is capable of controlling the proprietary service interfaces of most providers, and some cloud providers already have it in place. The basic XACML usage model assumes that when a resource access is attempted, a Policy Enforcement Point (PEP),

---

[14] Originally named as an acronym for the Simple Object Access Protocol.

responsible for protecting access to resources, sends a request containing a description of the attempted access to a Policy Decision Point (PDP) for evaluation against available policies and attributes. The PDP evaluates this request and returns an authorization decision for the PEP to enforce. XACML does not define protocols or transport mechanisms or specify how user credentials are validated. Messages transmitted between XACML entities are susceptible to attack by malicious third parties, including unauthorized disclosure, replay, deletion and modification attacks, unless sufficient safeguards are in place to protect transactions [Kel05].

4.6 Software Isolation

High degrees of multi-tenancy over large numbers of platforms are needed for cloud computing to achieve the envisioned flexibility of on-demand provisioning of reliable services and the cost benefits and efficiencies due to economies of scale. To reach the high scales of consumption desired, cloud providers have to ensure dynamic, flexible delivery of service and isolation of consumer resources. Multi-tenancy in IaaS cloud computing environments is typically done by multiplexing the execution of virtual machines from potentially different consumers on the same physical server [Ris09]. Applications deployed on guest virtual machines remain susceptible to attack and compromise, much the same as their non-virtualized counterparts. This was dramatically exemplified by a botnet found operating out of an IaaS cloud computing environment [Mcm09a, Whi09].

Multi-tenancy in PaaS and SaaS cloud computing environments can be handled differently. For example, many SaaS providers rely on an infrastructure free of virtual machines, using instead a single logical instance of an application (i.e., a software technology stack) that can handle extremely large numbers of tenants, scaling upwards or outwards as needed [Arm10, Wai08]. Regardless of the service model and multi-tenant software architecture used, the computations of different consumers must be able to be carried out in isolation from one another, mainly through the use of logical separation mechanisms.

- **Hypervisor Complexity.** The security of a computer system depends on the quality of the underlying software kernel that controls the confinement and execution of processes. A virtual machine monitor or hypervisor is designed to run multiple virtual machines, each hosting an operating system and applications, concurrently on a single host computer, and to provide isolation between the different guest virtual machines.

  A virtual machine monitor can, in theory, be smaller and less complex than an operating system. These characteristics generally make it easier to analyze and improve the quality of security, giving a virtual machine monitor the potential to be better suited for maintaining strong isolation between guest virtual machines than an operating system is for isolating processes [Kar08]. In practice, however, modern hypervisors can be large and complex, comparable to an operating system, which negates this advantage. For example, Xen, an open source x86 virtual machine monitor, incorporates a modified Linux kernel to implement a privileged partition for input/output operations, and KVM, another open source effort, transforms a Linux kernel into a virtual machine monitor [Kar08, Sha08, Xen08]. Understanding the use of virtualization by a cloud provider is a prerequisite to understanding the security risk involved.

- **Attack Vectors.** Multi-tenancy in virtual machine-based cloud infrastructures, together with the subtleties in the way physical resources are shared between guest virtual machines, can give rise to new sources of threat. The most serious threat is that malicious code can escape the confines of its virtual machine and interfere with the hypervisor or other guest virtual machines. Live migration, the ability to transition a virtual machine between hypervisors on different host computers without halting the guest operating system, and other features provided by virtual machine monitor environments to facilitate systems management, also increase software size and complexity and potentially add other areas to target in an attack.

Several examples illustrate the types of attack vectors possible. The first is mapping the cloud infrastructure. While seemingly a daunting task to perform, researchers have demonstrated an approach with a popular IaaS cloud [Ris09]. By launching multiple virtual machine instances from multiple cloud consumer accounts and using network probes, assigned IP addresses and domain names were analyzed to identify service location patterns. Building on that information and general technique, the plausible location of a specific target virtual machine could be identified and new virtual machines instantiated to be eventually co-resident with the target.

Once a suitable target location is found, the next step for the guest virtual machine is to bypass or overcome containment by the hypervisor or to takedown the hypervisor and system entirely. Weaknesses in the provided programming interfaces and the processing of instructions are common targets for uncovering vulnerabilities to exploit [Fer07]. For example, a serious flaw that allowed an attacker to write to an arbitrary out-of-bounds memory location was discovered in the power management code of a hypervisor by fuzzing emulated I/O ports [Orm07].[15] A denial of service vulnerability, which could allow a guest virtual machine to crash the host computer along with the other virtual machines being hosted, was also uncovered in a virtual device driver of a popular virtualization software product [Vmw09].

More indirect attack avenues may also be possible. For example, researchers developed a way for an attacker to gain administrative control of guest virtual machines during a live migration, by employing a man-in-the-middle attack to modify the code used for authentication [Obe08a]. Memory modification during migration presents other possibilities, such as the potential to insert a virtual machine-based rootkit layer below the operating system [Kin06]. A zero-day exploit in HyperVM, an open source application for managing virtual private servers, purportedly led to the destruction of approximately 100,000 virtual server-based Websites hosted by a service provider [Goo09b]. Another example of an indirect attack involves monitoring resource utilization on a shared server to gain information and perhaps perform a side-channel attack, similar to attacks used against implementations of cryptographic mechanisms in

---

[15] Fuzzing is a type of fault injection technique that involves sending pseudorandom data to an interface to discover flaws.

other computing environments [Ris09]. For example, an attacker could determine periods of high activity, estimate high-traffic rates, and possibly launch keystroke timing attacks to gather passwords and other data from a target server.

4.7 Data Protection

Data stored in a public cloud typically resides in a shared environment collocated with data from other customers. Organizations placing sensitive and regulated data into a public cloud, therefore, must account for the means by which access to the data is controlled and the data is kept secure. Similar concerns exist for data migrated within or between clouds.

- **Value Concentration.** A response to the question "Why do you rob banks?" is often attributed to Willie Sutton, a historic and prolific bank robber [Coc97]—his purported answer: "because that is where the money is." In many ways, data records are the currency of the 21st century and cloud-based data stores are the bank vault, making them an increasingly preferred target due to the collective value concentrated there [Row07]. Just as economies of scale exist in robbing banks instead of individuals, a high payoff ratio also exists for successfully compromising a cloud. Successful exploits against highly regarded security firms illustrate that no one is beyond the reach of a determined adversary (e.g., [And11], [Bra11], and [Pep11b]).

  As opposed to a direct approach, Willie's trademark was a combination of finesse and circumvention. That style works as well in the digital world of cloud computing. For instance, a recent exploit involved targeting a personal electronic mail account of a social networking service administrator, reportedly by answering a set of security questions to gain access to the account, and using the information found there to gain access to company files stored in a PaaS cloud [Inf09, Sut09]. A similar weakness in password resets was identified in an IaaS public cloud [Gar07]. A registered electronic mail address and valid password for an account were all that were required to download authentication credentials from the cloud provider's management dashboard, which in turn granted access to all of the account's resources. Since lost passwords for the cloud service could be reset by electronic mail, an attacker controlling the mail system associated with an account, or passively eavesdropping on the network through which electronic mail containing a password reset would pass, could effectively take control of the account.

  Having data collocated with that of an organization with a high threat profile could also lead to a denial of service, as an unintended casualty from an attack targeted against that organization [Row07]. Similarly, side effects from a physical attack against a high profile organization's cloud-based resources are also a possibility. For example, over the years, facilities of the Internal Revenue Service have attracted their share of attention from would-be attackers [Kat10, Lab95, Lat96, Sch10].

- **Data Isolation.** Data can take many forms. For example, for cloud-based application development, it includes the application programs, scripts, and configuration settings, along with the development tools. For deployed applications, it includes records and other content created or used by the applications, including deallocated objects, as well as

29

account information about the users of the applications. Access controls are one means to keep data away from unauthorized users; encryption is another. Access controls are typically identity-based, which makes authentication of the user's identity an important issue in cloud computing. Lacking physical control over the storage of information, encryption is the only way to ensure that it is truly protected.

Database environments used in cloud computing can vary significantly. For example, some environments support a multi-instance model, while others support a multi-tenant model. The former provide a unique database management system running on a virtual machine instance for each cloud consumer, giving the consumer complete control over role definition, user authorization, and other administrative tasks related to security. The latter provide a predefined environment for the cloud consumer that is shared with other tenants, typically through tagging data with a consumer identifier. Tagging gives the appearance of exclusive use of the instance, but relies on the cloud provider to establish and maintain a sound secure database environment.

Various types of multi-tenant arrangements exist for databases. Each arrangement pools resources differently, offering different degrees of isolation and resource efficiency [Jac07, Wai08]. Other considerations also apply. For example, certain features, like data encryption, are more viable with arrangements that use separate rather than shared databases. These sorts of tradeoffs require careful evaluation of the suitability of the data management solution for the data involved. Requirements in certain fields or industries, such as healthcare, would likely influence the choice of database and data organization used in an application. Privacy sensitive information, in general, is a serious concern [Pea09].

Data must be secured while at rest, in transit, and in use, and access to the data must be controlled. Standards for communications protocols and public key certificates allow data transfers to be protected using cryptography and can usually be implemented with equal effort in SaaS, PaaS, and IaaS environments [CSA11a, Pro10]. Procedures for protecting data at rest are not as well standardized, however, making interoperability an issue due to the predominance of proprietary systems. Capabilities also vary greatly across service models, and cryptographic protection may not be feasible for some environments, particularly PaaS and SaaS environments [CSA11a, Pro10]. The lack of interoperability affects the availability of data and complicates the portability of applications and data between cloud providers. Protecting data in use is an emerging area of cryptography with little practical results to offer, leaving trust mechanisms as the main safeguard [Gre09, Pro10].

The security of a system employing cryptography depends on the proper control of central keys and key management components [Bar05]. Currently, the responsibility for cryptographic key management falls mainly on the cloud consumer. Key generation and storage is usually performed outside the cloud using hardware security modules, which do not scale well to the cloud paradigm. NIST's Cryptographic Key Management Project is identifying scalable and usable cryptographic key management and exchange strategies for use by government, which could help to alleviate the problem eventually.[16]

A guiding principle is for employees of the organization to be in control of the central keying material and to configure the key management components for cloud-based applications [Bar05]. Before proceeding in cloud environments where the cloud provider provides facilities for key management, the organization must fully understand and weigh the risks involved in the processes defined by the cloud provider for the key management lifecycle [SCA11]. Cryptographic operations performed in the cloud become part of the key management process and, therefore, should be managed and audited by the organization.

■ **Data Sanitization.** The data sanitization practices that a cloud provider implements have obvious implications for security. Sanitization involves the expunging of data from storage media by overwriting, degaussing, or other means, or the destruction of the media itself, to prevent unauthorized disclosure of information.[17] It applies in various equipment refresh or maintenance situations, such as when a storage device is removed from service or repurposed. Data sanitization also applies to backup copies made for recovery and restoration of service and residual data remaining upon termination of service.

In a public cloud computing environment, data from one consumer is physically collocated (e.g., in an IaaS data store) or commingled (e.g., in a SaaS database) with the data of other consumers, which can complicate matters. Many examples exist of researchers obtaining used drives from online auctions and other sources and recovering large amounts of sensitive information from them (e.g., [Val08]). With the proper skills and equipment, it is also possible to recover data from failed drives, if they are not disposed of properly [Sob06]. Service agreements should stipulate sufficient measures that are taken to ensure data sanitization is performed appropriately throughout the system lifecycle.

4.8 Availability

In simple terms, availability is the extent to which an organization's full set of computational resources is accessible and usable. Availability can be affected temporarily or permanently, and a loss can be partial or complete. Denial of service attacks, equipment outages, and natural disasters are all threats to availability. The concern is that most downtime is unplanned and can impact the mission of the organization.

■ **Temporary Outages.** Despite employing architectures designed for high service reliability and availability, cloud computing services can and do experience outages and

---

[16] Cryptographic Key Management Project Website - http://csrc.nist.gov/groups/ST/key_mgmt/

[17] For more detailed information about sanitization, see Guidelines for Media Sanitization - http://csrc.nist.gov/publications/nistpubs/800-88/NISTSP800-88_rev1.pdf.

performance slowdowns [Lea09]. A number of examples illustrate this point. In February 2008, a popular storage cloud service suffered a three-hour outage that affected its consumers, including Twitter and other startup companies [Dig08, Kri08, Mil08]. In June 2009, a lightning storm caused a partial outage of an IaaS cloud that affected some users for four hours, and in April 2011, a network upgrade attempt caused a serous outage lasting more than twenty-four hours [Met11, Mil09, Pep11a]. Similarly, in February 2008, a database cluster failure at a SaaS cloud caused an outage for several hours, and in January 2009, another brief outage occurred due to a network device failure [Fer09, Goo09a, Mod08]. In March 2009, a PaaS cloud experienced severe degradation for about twenty-two hours due to networking issues related to an upgrade [Cla09, Mic09].

At a level of 99.95% availability, 4.38 hours of downtime are to be expected in a year. Periods of scheduled maintenance are usually excluded as a source of downtime in SLAs and may be scheduled with short notice from the cloud provider. The level of availability of a cloud service and its capabilities for data backup and disaster recovery need to be addressed in the organization's contingency and continuity planning to ensure the recovery and restoration of disrupted cloud services and operations, using alternate services, equipment, and locations, if required. Cloud storage services may represent a single point of failure for the applications hosted there. In such situations, the services of a second cloud provider could be used to back up data processed by the primary provider to ensure that during a prolonged disruption or serious disaster at the primary's facilities, the data remains available for immediate resumption of critical operations.

- **Prolonged and Permanent Outages.** The possibility exists for a cloud provider to experience serious problems, like bankruptcy or facility loss, which affect service for extended periods or cause a complete shutdown. For example, in April 2009, the Federal Bureau of Investigation raided computing centers in Texas and seized hundreds of servers, when investigating fraud allegations against a handful of companies that operated out of the centers [Zet09a]. The seizure disrupted service to hundreds of other businesses unrelated to the investigation, but who had the misfortune of having their computer operations collocated at the targeted centers [Zet09a]. A similar raid with much the same result occurred more recently [Sch11]. Other examples of outages are the major data loss experienced in 2009 by a bookmark repository service, and the abrupt failure of an on-line storage-as-a-service provider, who closed without warning to its users in 2008 [Cal09, Gun08]. Changing business conditions may also cause a cloud provider to disband its services, as occurred recently with an online cloud storage service [Sto10].

If an organization relies on a cloud service for data storage and processing, it must be prepared to carry on mission critical operations without the use of the service for periods when the cloud experiences a serious outage. The organization's contingency plan should address prolonged and permanent system disruptions and support continuity of operations that effect the restoration of essential functions elsewhere. Having policy, plans, and standard operating procedures in place avoids creating an undue reliance on employing cloud services without sufficient recourse.

- **Denial of Service.** A denial of service attack involves saturating the target with bogus requests to prevent it from responding to legitimate requests in a timely manner. An attacker typically uses multiple computers or a botnet to launch an assault. Even an unsuccessful distributed denial of service attack can quickly consume large amounts of resources to defend against and cause charges to soar. The dynamic provisioning of a cloud in some ways simplifies the work of an attacker to cause harm. While the resources of a cloud are significant, with enough attacking computers they can become saturated [Jen09]. For example, a denial of service attack against a code hosting site operating over an IaaS cloud resulted in more than 19 hours of downtime [Bro09, Met09].

  In addition to attacks against publicly available services accessible via the Internet, denial of service attacks can occur against internally accessible services, such as those used in cloud management [Mee09, Sla09]. Internally assigned non-routable addresses, used to manage resources within a cloud provider's network, may also be used as an attack vector. A worst-case possibility that exists is for elements of one cloud to attack those of another or to attack some of its own elements [Jen09].

4.9 Incident Response

As the name implies, incident response involves an organized method for dealing with the consequences of an attack against the security of a computer system. The cloud provider's role is vital in performing incident response activities, including incident verification, attack analysis, containment, data collection and preservation, problem remediation, and service restoration. Each layer in a cloud application stack, including the application, operating system, network, and database, generates event logs, as do other cloud components, such as load balancers and intrusion detection systems; many such event sources and the means of accessing them are under the control of the cloud provider.

The complexity of a cloud service can obscure recognition and analysis of incidents. For example, it reportedly took one IaaS provider approximately eight hours to recognize and begin taking action on an apparent denial of service attack against its cloud infrastructure, after the issue was reported by a consumer of the service [Bro09, Met09]. Revising an organization's incident response plan to address differences between the organizational computing environment and a cloud computing environment is an important, but easy-to-overlook prerequisite to transitioning applications and data.

- **Data Availability.** The availability of relevant data from event monitoring is essential for timely detection of security incidents. Cloud consumers are often confronted with extremely limited capabilities for detection of incidents in public cloud environments [Gro10]. Prominent issues include insufficient access to event sources and vulnerability information under the control of the cloud provider, inadequate interfaces for accessing and processing event data automatically, inability to add detection points within the cloud infrastructure, and difficulty directing third-party reported abuses and incidents effectively back to the correct consumer or the cloud provider for handling. The situation varies among cloud service models and cloud providers [Gro10]. For example, PaaS providers typically do not make event logs available to consumers, who are then left

33

mainly with event data from self-deployed applications (e.g., via application logging). Similarly, SaaS consumers are completely dependent upon the cloud provider to provide event data such as activity logging, while IaaS consumers control more of the information stack and have access to associated event sources.

- **Incident Analysis and Resolution.** An analysis to confirm the occurrence of an incident or determine the method of exploit needs to be performed quickly and with sufficient detail of documentation and care to ensure that traceability and integrity is maintained for subsequent use, if needed (e.g., a forensic copy of incident data for legal proceedings) [Gro10]. To gain a full understanding of an incident, the scope of affected networks, systems, and applications must be determined, the intrusion vector must be uncovered, and the activities carried out must be reconstructed [Gro10]. Issues faced by cloud consumers when performing incident analysis include lack of detailed information about the architecture of the cloud relevant to an incident, lack of information about relevant event and data sources held by the cloud provider, ill-defined or vague incident handling responsibilities stipulated for the cloud provider, and limited capabilities for gathering and preserving pertinent data sources as evidence.

  Once the scope of the incident and the assets affected are determined, measures can be taken to contain and resolve the incident, bringing systems back to a secure operational state [Gro10]. The roles and responsibilities between the cloud provider and cloud consumer for containing an attack vary based on the service model and cloud architecture. For example, in SaaS and PaaS cloud environments, containment essentially amounts to reducing or removing the functionality (e.g., by filtering out certain users or features with a web application firewall) that the attacker is using to carry out unauthorized activities, if necessary, taking the entire application off-line [Gro10]. In IaaS cloud environments, the cloud consumer has a more prominent role; however, the cloud provider's assistance is essential to resolve vulnerabilities exploited in the underlying cloud infrastructure.

Response to an incident should be handled in a way that limits damage and minimizes recovery time and costs. Collaboration between the cloud consumer and provider in recognizing and responding to an incident is vital to security and privacy in cloud computing. Federal agencies have an obligation to report certain categories of incidents to the U.S. Computer Emergency Readiness Team (US-CERT) within one or two hours of discovery or detection.[18] A clear understanding is needed of the type of incidents that are reportable by the cloud provider (e.g., data breaches) versus those that are not reportable (e.g., intrusion detection alarms). Remedies may involve only a single party or require the participation of both parties. Being able to convene a mixed team of representatives from the cloud provider and cloud consumer quickly is an important facet of an efficient and cost-effective response.

---

[18] For more information, see http://www.us-cert.gov/federal/reportingRequirements.html.

For an incident response team to perform effectively, it must be able to act autonomously and decisively. The resolution of a problem may impact many consumers of the cloud service. It is important that cloud providers have a transparent response process and mechanisms to share information with their consumers during and after the incident. Understanding and negotiating the provisions and procedures for incident response should be done before entering into a service contract, rather than as an afterthought. For example, incident response plans should address breaches involving PII and ways to minimize the amount of PII involved when reporting and responding to a breach [Mcc10]. The geographic location of data is a related issue that can impede an investigation, and is a relevant subject for contract discussions.

4.10 Summary of Recommendations

A number of significant security and privacy issues were covered in the previous subsections. Table 1 summarizes those issues and related recommendations for organizations to follow when planning, reviewing, negotiating, or initiating a public cloud service outsourcing arrangement.

Table 1: Security and Privacy Issues and Recommendations

Areas	Recommendations
Governance	Extend organizational practices pertaining to the policies, procedures, and standards used for application development and service provisioning in the cloud, as well as the design, implementation, testing, use, and monitoring of deployed or engaged services.
	Put in place audit mechanisms and tools to ensure organizational practices are followed throughout the system lifecycle.
Compliance	Understand the various types of laws and regulations that impose security and privacy obligations on the organization and potentially impact cloud computing initiatives, particularly those involving data location, privacy and security controls, records management, and electronic discovery requirements.
	Review and assess the cloud provider's offerings with respect to the organizational requirements to be met and ensure that the contract terms adequately meet the requirements.
	Ensure that the cloud provider's electronic discovery capabilities and processes do not compromise the privacy or security of data and applications.
Trust	Ensure that service arrangements have sufficient means to allow visibility into the security and privacy controls and processes employed by the cloud provider, and their performance over time.
	Establish clear, exclusive ownership rights over data.
	Institute a risk management program that is flexible enough to adapt to the constantly evolving and shifting risk landscape for the lifecycle of the system.
	Continuously monitor the security state of the information system to support on-going risk management decisions.

Areas	Recommendations
Architecture	Understand the underlying technologies that the cloud provider uses to provision services, including the implications that the technical controls involved have on the security and privacy of the system, over the full system lifecycle and across all system components.
Identity and Access Management	Ensure that adequate safeguards are in place to secure authentication, authorization, and other identity and access management functions, and are suitable for the organization.
Software Isolation	Understand virtualization and other logical isolation techniques that the cloud provider employs in its multi-tenant software architecture, and assess the risks involved for the organization.
Data Protection	Evaluate the suitability of the cloud provider's data management solutions for the organizational data concerned and the ability to control access to data, to secure data while at rest, in transit, and in use, and to sanitize data. Take into consideration the risk of collating organizational data with that of other organizations whose threat profiles are high or whose data collectively represent significant concentrated value. Fully understand and weigh the risks involved in cryptographic key management with the facilities available in the cloud environment and the processes established by the cloud provider.
Availability	Understand the contract provisions and procedures for availability, data backup and recovery, and disaster recovery, and ensure that they meet the organization's continuity and contingency planning requirements. Ensure that during an intermediate or prolonged disruption or a serious disaster, critical operations can be immediately resumed, and that all operations can be eventually reinstituted in a timely and organized manner.
Incident Response	Understand the contract provisions and procedures for incident response and ensure that they meet the requirements of the organization. Ensure that the cloud provider has a transparent response process in place and sufficient mechanisms to share information during and after an incident. Ensure that the organization can respond to incidents in a coordinated fashion with the cloud provider in accordance with their respective roles and responsibilities for the computing environment.

5. Public Cloud Outsourcing

Although cloud computing is a new computing paradigm, outsourcing information technology services is not. The steps that organizations take remain basically the same for public clouds as with other, more traditional, information technology services, and existing guidelines for outsourcing generally apply as well. What does change with public cloud computing, however, is the potential for increased complexity and difficulty in providing adequate oversight to maintain accountability and control over deployed applications and systems throughout their lifecycle. This can be especially daunting if the terms of the service agreement do not fully meet the needs of the organization, since responsibilities normally held by the organization are given over to the cloud provider and, without sufficient provisions, the organization would have little recourse to address problems and resolve to its satisfaction issues that may arise. That is, the service agreement is the primary means for an organization to enforce control and maintain accountability over the computing environment. If any needed requirements or sureties are missing, accountability is threatened accordingly.

The record for traditional information technology outsourcing is mixed with respect to security and privacy, and not consistently done well by federal agencies (e.g., [GAO06, GAO10]). As discussed in the previous chapter, transitioning organizational data and functions into a public cloud is accompanied by a host of security and privacy issues to be addressed, many of which concern the adequacy of the cloud provider's technical controls for an organization's needs. Service arrangements defined in the terms of service must also meet the privacy policy of the organization and the prevailing laws and regulations for information protection, dissemination, and disclosure to which the organization must comply. Each cloud provider and service arrangement has distinct costs and risks associated with it. A decision based on any one issue can have major implications for the organization in other areas [Gra03].

Considering the growing number of public cloud providers and the broad range of services offered by them, organizations must exercise due diligence when selecting and moving functions to a public cloud. Decision making about services and service arrangements entails striking a balance between benefits in cost and productivity versus drawbacks in risk and liability. While the sensitivity of data handled by government organizations and the current state of the art make the likelihood of outsourcing all information technology services to a public cloud low, it should be possible for most government organizations to deploy some of their information technology services to a public cloud, provided that all requisite risk mitigations are taken.

> **Cloud Transition Case Study:** The City of Los Angeles' initiative to move to cloud computing provides insight to the planning involved and the issues that can arise [CSC10]. The effort involves switching the city's electronic mail and calendaring system from an on-site solution to a public SaaS cloud that provides those services, and adding capabilities to improve productivity and collaboration [CSC10, DPW10, SECS09]. User training and electronic mail migration are also part of the contracted effort, which the City entered into on November 20, 2009.
>
> In its analysis of the proposed contract [CAO09], the Office of the City Administrative Officer gave a qualified recommendation to proceed, noting that *"If the City decides to utilize*

these services..., it may be cost prohibitive to return to the current City-owned and operated structure." The analysis also cautioned that *"Several findings in this report, including the fact that the proposed system costs more than the current system, the potential operational impact from stopping the use of Microsoft Office, the shift in control over the City's e-mail and office applications to an outside vendor, and uncertainty surrounding security issues, illustrate the potential risks of approving this contract."*

The City of Los Angeles was able to negotiate a number of security and privacy-related items into the SaaS E-mail and Collaboration Solution (SECS) contract that would be of interest to most government agencies [CSC10, Ove10, Wil10]. For example, the police and fire departments expressed concern that arrest records and other sensitive criminal data they handle could be vulnerable when maintained on external servers. This resulted in the requirement to protect the City's data through mandatory encryption, segregation from other data maintained by the cloud provider, and constraints on data storage location [LAPD10, Wil10]. As an added measure, the cloud provider's employees who have access to the City's data must pass background checks by the California Department of Justice.

Other important negotiated features include on-site audit rights of the contractor's security program, service level requirements with monetary penalties, electronic discovery functionality, well-defined data ownership and exit rights, mandatory subcontractor flow-down, and a broad indemnification obligation with unlimited liability for certain breaches [Ove10, SECS09, Wil10]. Data remains permanently the sole and exclusive property of the City [Cra10]. The cloud provider requires written approval from the City to open any files in the clear; all accesses are logged and the City has a means to self-audit accesses [Cra10].

As with nearly all software changeovers, training, integration, data migration, and other related issues exist and their impact on productivity should not be underestimated or discounted when planning cloud computing initiatives [Mic10]. For example, there were some striking differences in features between L.A.'s legacy electronic mail services and those of the SaaS [DPW10]: the cloud provider's mail service did not support classifying outgoing electronic mail with High, Standard, and Low priority; it also did not support a feature to track replies from recipients; nor did it support the use of folders to organize email, relying instead on labels. City employees were also required to carry out important migration-related tasks that include such things as cleaning up existing mail accounts by deleting all unimportant electronic mail and canceled appointments; archiving all mail by year; and individually saving any mail attachments larger than 25 megabytes, since they would not be automatically migrated to the new system [DPW10].

The security of sensitive data from the police department and other city agencies proved to be a more difficult requirement to satisfy than thought originally, and caused a delay in implementation [CLA10, LAPD10, Sar10]. Because of the delay, the legacy system continued to operate in parallel with the replacement system longer than originally planned and at additional cost, until a solution could be put into place. Hundreds of police department accounts that were switched over to the new system had to be restored to the legacy system in the interim. The Director of Operations for the cloud provider noted: *"LA's move to the cloud is the first of its kind, and it's not surprising that it's taken a little longer than anticipated to identify and address all of the City's unique requirements"* [Din10].

In December 2010, the City of LA issued a Notice of Deficiencies to the contractor raising concerns about the failure of the system to meet all security requirements and its impact on City departments [CWD10, Vij11]. In April 2011, it was reported that if this issue was not resolved by June 2011, the end of the fiscal year, City officials would consider terminating the agreement, and possibly look into whether a breach of contract occurred [Sar11a, Vij11].

As of August 22, 2011, the majority of users had been successfully migrated to the replacement system. While the LA police department remained on the legacy system because of security concerns, expectations were that all outstanding issues would be resolved by the first quarter of 2012 and that the department would complete its migration [Cra11]. That timeline would give the City about eight months to decide whether to continue the service into the first option year of the contract (i.e., the fourth year), or to seek an alternative solution.

On December 14, 2011, the Los Angeles City Council voted to scale back the SECS contract, concluding that the security needs of crucial departments were not able to be met by the cloud provider [CLA11a, CLA11b, Gou11, Sar11b]. The police department, fire department, and city attorney's office are among the departments excepted. The cloud provider also agreed to pay the costs of the legacy system during the term of the contract and any extensions of the contract.

5.1 General Concerns

The terms of traditional information technology outsourcing contracts, particularly those involving sensitive data, can serve as guidelines for cloud computing initiatives. Three main security and privacy issues in service contracts have been identified previously and are relevant to outsourcing public cloud computing services [All88, Len03]:

- **Inadequate Policies and Practices.** The security policies and practices of the cloud provider might not be adequate or compatible with those of the organization. The same issue applies to privacy as well. This can result in complications such as the following [All88]:

  - Undetected intrusions or violations due to insufficient auditing and monitoring policies by the cloud provider
  - Lack of sufficient data and configuration integrity due to a mismatch between the organization's and the cloud provider's policies for separation of duty (i.e., clear assignment of roles and responsibilities) or redundancy (i.e., having sufficient checks and balances to ensure an operation is done consistently and correctly)
  - Loss of privacy due to the cloud provider handling sensitive information less rigorously than the organization's policy dictates.

- **Weak Confidentiality and Integrity Sureties.** Insufficient security controls in the cloud provider's platform could affect negatively the confidentiality and privacy, or integrity of the system. For example, use of an insecure method of remote access could allow intruders to gain unauthorized access, modify, or destroy the organization's information systems and resources; to deliberately introduce security vulnerabilities or malware into the system; or to launch attacks on other systems from the organization's network, perhaps making the organization liable for the damages incurred [All88].

- **Weak Availability Sureties.** Insufficient safeguards in the cloud provider's platform could negatively affect the availability of the system. Besides the applications directly affected, a loss of system availability may cause a conflict for key resources that are required for critical organizational operations. For example, if disruptive processing operations (e.g., load rebalancing due to site failure or emergency maintenance) are performed by the cloud provider at the same time as peak organizational processing occurs, a denial of service condition could arise [All88]. A denial of service attack targeted at the cloud provider could also affect the organization's applications and systems operating in the cloud or at the organization's data center.

Assurances furnished to the organization by the cloud provider to support security claims, or by a certification and compliance review entity paid by the cloud provider, should be verified whenever possible through independent assessment by the organization. Moreover, a third-party certification or other assurances from the cloud provider do not necessarily grant a tenant application or system that same level of certification or compliance; those elements would likely require a separate certification assessment for that specific cloud environment.[19]

Other noteworthy concerns, which are indirectly related to security and privacy, also exist with outsourcing to public clouds. One of the most prevalent and challenging concerns is called the principal-agent problem. Another is the attenuation of an organization's technical expertise.

- **Principal-Agent Problem.** The principal-agent problem occurs when the incentives of the agent (i.e., the cloud provider) are not aligned with the interests of the principal (i.e., the organization) [Row07]. Because it can be difficult to determine the level of effort a cloud provider is exerting towards security and privacy administration and remediation, the concern is that the organization might not recognize if the service level is dropping or has dropped below the extent required. One confounding issue is that increased security efforts are not guaranteed to result in noticeable improvements (e.g., fewer incidents), in part because of the growing amounts of malware and new types of attacks [Row07].

- **Attenuation of Expertise.** Outsourced computing services can, over time, diminish the level of technical knowledge and expertise of the organization, since management and staff no longer need to deal regularly with technical issues at a detailed level [Gon09]. As new advancements and improvements are made to the cloud computing environment, the knowledge and expertise gained directly benefit the cloud provider, not the organization. Unless precautions are taken, an organization can lose its ability to keep up to date with technology advances and related security and privacy considerations, which in turn can affect its ability to plan and oversee new information technology projects effectively and to maintain accountability over existing cloud-based systems.

An organization may be able to employ compensating security and privacy controls to work around identified shortcomings in a public cloud service. Non-negotiable service agreements generally limit the range of risk-mitigation activities available to an organization, while

---

[19] The Federal Risk and Authorization Management Program has been established to provide a standard approach to assessing and authorizing cloud computing services and products that results in a joint authorization of cloud providers with respect to a common security risk model. The joint authorization issued can be reused and leveraged and across the Federal Government in cloud computing deployments for which the security risk model applies - http://www.cio.gov/modules/fedramp/demo.cfm.

negotiated service agreements, which provide greater range and flexibility, necessitate careful scrutiny and prioritization of requirements that are incorporated into the terms of service in order to be cost effective. In either case, however, available risk mitigation techniques are unlikely to ever be sufficient enough to allow high-value or highly sensitive data or mission-critical applications to be deployed to a public cloud. For these situations, the organization could consider employing a cloud computing environment with a more suitable deployment model, such as an internal private cloud, which can potentially offer greater oversight and authority over security and privacy, and better limit the type of tenants that share platform resources, reducing exposure in the event of a failure or configuration error in a control.

There are several distinct stages of outsourcing at which an organization can carry out prescribed activities to remain accountable and mitigate the above-mentioned security and privacy issues: when planning the initiative (i.e., preliminary activities), when initiating the service contract and overseeing it (i.e., initiating and coincident activities), and when closing down the services and contract (i.e., concluding activities) [All88, Len03]. The subsequent sections of this chapter discuss these stages in detail.

Federal Information Processing Standards (FIPS) are pertinent to all stages of outsourcing, particularly FIPS 199 and FIPS 200, which apply to planning at the early stages.[20]

- **FIPS 199.** This standard, entitled Standards for Security Categorization of Federal Information and Information Systems, provides a common framework and method for categorizing information and information systems to ensure that adequate levels of information security are provided, which are commensurate with the level of risk. The resulting security categorization feeds into other activities such as security control selection, privacy impact analysis, and critical infrastructure analysis.

- **FIPS 200.** This standard, entitled Minimum Security Requirements for Federal Information and Information Systems, directs agencies to meet the identified minimum security requirements for federal information and information systems by selecting the appropriate security controls and assurance requirements described in NIST Special Publication (SP) 800-53 Revision 3.

In addition to SP 800-53 mentioned above, other NIST guidelines provide information and guidance on planning, implementing, and managing information system security and protecting information that apply to outsourcing initiatives. They include the NIST SPs listed below in Table 2, whose principles have the utmost relevance to cloud computing environments overall and should be used in conjunction with this publication.[21]

---

[20] For information about F Publications, see NIST's FIPS Home Page - http://itl.nist.gov/fipspubs/.

[21] For information about these NIST guidelines, as well as other security-related publications, see NIST's Web page - http://csrc.nist.gov/publications/index.html.

Table 2: Selected NIST Special Publications

Publication No.	Title
SP 800-18	Guide for Developing Security Plans for Federal Information Systems
SP 800-34, Revision 1	Contingency Planning Guide for Federal Information Systems
SP 800-37, Revision 1	Guide for Applying the Risk Management Framework to Federal Information Systems
SP 800-39	Managing Information Security Risk
SP 800-53, Revision 3	Recommended Security Controls for Federal Information Systems and Organizations
SP 800-53, Appendix J	Privacy Control Catalog
SP 800-53A, Revision 1	Guide for Assessing the Security Controls in Federal Information Systems
SP 800-60	Guide for Mapping Types of Information and Information Systems to Security Categories
SP 800-61, Revision 1	Computer Security Incident Handling Guide
SP 800-64, Revision 2	Security Considerations in the System Development Life Cycle
SP 800-86	Guide to Integrating Forensic Techniques into Incident Response
SP 800-88	Guidelines for Media Sanitization
SP 800-115	Technical Guide to Information Security Testing and Assessment
SP 800-122	Guide to Protecting the Confidentiality of Personally Identifiable Information (PII)
SP 800-137	Information Security Continuous Monitoring for Federal Information Systems and Organizations

In accordance with OMB policy, federal agencies are required to follow certain specific NIST Special Publications. However, there is flexibility in how agencies apply the guidance. Federal agencies should apply the security concepts and principles articulated in the NIST Special Publications in accordance with and in the context of the agency's missions, business functions, and environment of operation. Consequently, the application of NIST guidance by federal agencies can result in different security solutions that are equally acceptable, compliant with the guidance, and meet the OMB definition of adequate security for federal information systems.

5.2 Preliminary Activities

In the first stage of outsourcing, the organization must perform various planning activities in preparation for issuing a contract for public cloud services. Planning helps to ensure that an organization derives full benefit from information technology spending. It also helps to ensure that the computing environment is as secure as possible and in compliance with all relevant organizational policies and that data privacy is maintained. Planning activities include the following items:

- **Specify Requirements.** The organization must identify its security, privacy, and other requirements for cloud services, as a criterion for the selection of a cloud provider. Common security requirements include coverage for the following areas [CSA11b, Len03]:

  - Personnel requirements, including clearances, roles, and responsibilities
  - Regulatory requirements
  - Service availability
  - Problem reporting, review, and resolution
  - Information handling and disclosure agreements and procedures
  - Physical and logical access controls
  - Network access control, connectivity, and filtering
  - Data protection
  - System configuration and patch management
  - Backup and recovery
  - Data retention and sanitization
  - Security and vulnerability scanning
  - Risk management
  - Incident reporting, handling, and response
  - Continuity of operations
  - Resource management
  - Certification and accreditation
  - Assurance levels
  - Independent auditing of services.

Part of the requirements analysis should narrow the choice among IaaS, PaaS, and SaaS service models to a single selection that is appropriate for the agency's specific needs and objectives. The responsibilities of both the organization and the cloud provider vary depending on the service model. For example in IaaS, the cloud provider's responsibility typically stops at the hypervisor. Organizations consuming cloud services must understand the delineation of responsibilities and how they must tie into the cloud provider's processes to ensure that organizational governance practices are extended over this environment, and that mechanisms and tools are provided for managing those aspects that fall under the organization's responsibility.

Establishing an exit strategy is an important part of the planning process and should be factored into the requirements analysis. It also relates to the organization's contingency and continuity planning activities. The exit strategy should cover a normal termination, such as that at expiration of the service agreement, and also an unexpected termination, such as that due to service provider bankruptcy or poor performance [Gra03]. The ability to export all of the organization's data in a usable format through a secure, reliable, and efficient means, and in a timely manner, is a vital aspect of an exit strategy. Other aspects include addressing application dependencies on proprietary programming interfaces, system calls, and database technologies, as well as the recovery of useful metadata that may have accumulated within the cloud environment.

Compliance with various federal standards, OMB guidance, and public law imposes requirements that need to be addressed in the requirement analysis. The implications of some key laws and regulations were discussed in the previous chapter, but others abound. For example, if a public-facing aspect to the cloud implementation exists, OMB Memoranda M-10-22, Guidance for Online Use of Web Measurement and Customization Technologies, and M-10-23, Guidance for Agency Use of Third-Party Websites and Applications, provide compliance guidance in terms of branding, PIA, policy, and other issues to be considered during planning. Compliance-related requirements, such as the protection of PII, may also be specific to an agency [Mcc10].[22] Other requirements relevant to outsourcing exist, such as records management controls, accessibility, and user training, and should also be addressed. For example, Section 508 of the Rehabilitation Act of 1973 (29 U.S.C. 794d) establishes electronic and information technology requirements for accessibility to people with disabilities, including employees and members of the public.

Reviewing common outsourcing provisions in existing cloud computing contracts that cover areas such as privacy and security standards, regulatory and compliance issues, service level criteria and penalties, change management processes, continuity of service provisions, and termination rights, can be helpful in formulating requirements [Ove10]. Existing information technology outsourcing contracts in use by the organization can also be helpful.

Fair Information Practice Principles. Fair Information Practices, also known as Privacy Principles, are the framework for most modern privacy laws around the world [Mcc10]. The Organization for Economic Co-operation and Development (OECD), of which the U.S. is a member, adopted Guidelines on the Protection of Privacy and Transborder Flows of Personal Data in 1980 [OECD80]. The guidelines provide a framework for privacy that has been referenced in U.S. Federal guidance and also internationally, and can be used by federal agencies to formulate their requirements and address privacy concerns during planning. The guidelines specify the following eight privacy principles:

▪ *Collection Limitation.* There should be limits to the collection of personal data and any such data should be obtained by lawful and fair means and, where appropriate, with the knowledge or consent of the data subject.

▪ *Data Quality.* Personal data should be relevant to the purposes for which they are to be used and, to the extent necessary for those purposes, should be accurate, complete and kept up-to-date.

▪ *Purpose Specification.* The purposes for which personal data are collected should be specified not later than at the time of data collection and the subsequent use limited to the

---

[22] For example, the Veterans Affairs Information Security Enhancement Act, Title IX of P.L. 109-461, requires the Veterans Administration to implement agency-wide information security procedures to protect sensitive personal information (SPI) and information systems. SPI includes any information that is maintained about the individual, such as education, financial transactions, medical history, and criminal or employment history; and information that can be used to distinguish or trace the individual's identity, such as name, social security number, date and place of birth, mother's maiden name, and biometric records.

fulfillment of those purposes or such others as are not incompatible with those purposes and as are specified on each occasion of change of purpose.

- *Use Limitation.* Personal data should not be disclosed, made available or otherwise used for purposes other than those specified in accordance with the preceding principle except: with the consent of the data subject; or by the authority of law.

- *Security Safeguards.* Personal data should be protected by reasonable security safeguards against such risks as loss or unauthorized access, destruction, use, modification or disclosure of data.

- *Openness.* There should be a general policy of openness about developments, practices and policies with respect to personal data. Means should be readily available of establishing the existence and nature of personal data, and the main purposes of their use, as well as the identity and usual residence of the data controller.

- *Individual Participation.* An individual should have the right:
a) to obtain from a data controller, or otherwise, confirmation of whether or not the data controller has data relating to him;
b) to have communicated to him, data relating to him within a reasonable time; at a charge, if any, that is not excessive; in a reasonable manner; and in a form that is readily intelligible to him;
c) to be given reasons if a request made under subparagraphs(a) and (b) is denied, and to be able to challenge such denial; and
d) to challenge data relating to him and, if the challenge is successful to have the data erased, rectified, completed or amended.

- *Accountability.* A data controller should be accountable for complying with measures which give effect to the principles stated above.

Five core principles of privacy protection are also embodied in the Fair Information Practice Codes [FTC07]. They are similar to those in the OECD guidelines, but targeted toward commercial entities. Nevertheless, these principles provide a useful, supplemental perspective on privacy protection.

- *Notice/Awareness.* Consumers should be given notice of an entity's information practices before any personal information is collected to allow an informed decision to be made about what extent, if any, to disclose personal information. Notice of some or all of the following items are considered essential for ensuring that consumers are properly informed: identification of the entity collecting the data; identification of the uses to which the data will be put; identification of any potential recipients of the data; the nature of the data collected and the means by which it is collected if not obvious (e.g., passively, by means of electronic monitoring, or actively, by asking the consumer to supply the information); indication of whether the provision of the requested data is voluntary or required, and the consequences of a refusal to provide the requested information; and the steps taken to ensure the confidentiality, integrity and quality of the collected data.

- *Choice/Consent.* Choice means giving consumers options about the use of personal information that is collected. Choice relates specifically to secondary uses of information that go beyond those needed to carry out the contemplated transaction. Opt-in or opt-out are the two main types of choice/consent regimes. The former requires affirmation by the consumer to allow collection, while the latter requires affirmation to prevent it. Choice can also involve more than a binary option and allow consumers to tailor the type of the information they reveal and the acceptable uses for it.

• *Access/Participation.* Access refers to an individual's ability to review data held about him or herself and to contest that data's accuracy and completeness. The process should be simple, timely and inexpensive to the consumer, and allow consumer objections to be incorporated and sent to data recipients.

• *Integrity/Security.* Integrity requires that data be accurate and secure. To ensure integrity, reasonable measures should be in force, such as cross-referencing data against multiple sources for accuracy. Security involves measures to protect against loss and the unauthorized access, destruction, use, modification, and disclosure of data.

• *Enforcement/Redress.* Privacy protection can only be effective if there is a mechanism in place to enforce the core principles and remedy any undesirable or unfair situation with data that is collected. The data controller for whose benefit the processing of data is carried out should be accountable for meeting the core principles. Enforcement through industry self-regulation; legislation enabling private remedies for consumers; and regulatory schemes enforceable through civil and criminal sanctions are possibilities for redress.

■ **Assess Security and Privacy Risks.** While outsourcing relieves operational commitment on the part of the organization, the act of engaging public cloud services poses risks against which an organization needs to safeguard itself. The previous chapter stressed the importance of instituting a flexible and adaptable risk management program for the lifecycle of the system. The risk analysis carried out at this stage should include factors such as the service model involved, the purpose and scope of the service, the types and level of access needed by the provider and proposed for use between the organizational computing environment and provider services, the service duration and dependencies, and the strength of protection offered via the security controls available from the cloud provider [Len03]. Another consideration, if a non-negotiable service agreement applies, is whether the terms of service are subject to unilateral amendment by the cloud provider, which would increase the security and privacy risks involved [CIO10a]. Privacy controls should be assessed as part of the analysis, as well as operational risks due to the locations of the cloud provider's facilities.

An organization may require a Privacy Threshold Analysis (PTA) to be completed before the development or acquisition of a new information system and when a substantial change is made to an existing system [Mcc10]. PTAs are used to determine if a system contains PII, whether a PIA or a SORN is required, and whether other privacy requirements apply to the information system. As mentioned earlier, a PIA is normally conducted for all new or substantially changed technology that collects, maintains, or disseminates PII, and makes them publicly available.

PII should be evaluated to determine the potential harm that could result to the subject individuals and/or the organization if PII were inappropriately accessed, used, or disclosed (i.e., its confidentiality impact level) [Mcc10]. An organization decides upon the factors it uses in determining PII confidentiality impact levels and then creates and implements the appropriate policy, procedures, and controls to protect the information. For example, some federal agencies have expressed legal obligations to protect certain types of PII and should consider such obligations when determining the PII confidentiality impact levels and appropriate safeguards.[23]

The sensitivity of other types of data held by an organization is also an important factor when analyzing risk.[24] The range of data an organization deals with is sometimes not fully appreciated. While data repositories containing PII or classified information are more easily recognized and taken into account, pockets of other types of sensitive data with different rules for handling may also exist. They include data items such as the following:

- Law enforcement and investigative unit data
- System security information, such as network schematics, configuration settings, and vulnerability reports
- Licensed source code and libraries, used in application development
- Digital documents and materials obtained under a non-disclosure agreement or memorandum of agreement
- Laboratory and research data whose collection, storage, and sharing are regulated
- Culturally sensitive data related to resource protection and management of Indian tribal land.

An understanding of the underlying technologies the cloud provider uses to provision services is essential for conducting an accurate risk analysis. The security and privacy issues from the previous chapter identified important technology areas to review:

- Logical isolation techniques employed in the multi-tenant software architecture of the cloud
- Facilities for backup and recovery of data, and for sanitization of data
- Capabilities and processes for electronic discovery
- Mechanisms used to control access to data, to protect data while at rest, in transit, and in use, and to expunge data when no longer needed
- Facilities available for cryptography and cryptographic key management
- Mechanisms for secure authentication, authorization, and other identity and access management functions
- Facilities for incident response and disaster recovery.

As mentioned previously, if the results of a risk analysis show that the level is too high, the organization may be able to apply compensating controls to reduce risk to an acceptable level. Otherwise, it must either reject use of the service or accept a greater degree of risk. As an alternative to rejecting the service and not going forward, it might

---

[23] For information about determining PII confidentiality impact levels, see Guide to Protecting the Confidentiality of Personally Identifiable Information - http://csrc.nist.gov/publications/nistpubs/800-122/sp800-122.pdf

[24] The sensitivity of data from other organizations may also be a factor, if collocated with organizational data.

be possible to reduce the scope of the outsourcing effort to deal exclusively with less sensitive data. During a risk assessment, it also may become clear that some other model of deployment would be more suitable than a public cloud for the service model and application under analysis.

- **Assess the Competency of the Cloud Provider.** Before awarding a contract for outsourced services, the organization should evaluate the cloud provider's ability and commitment to deliver the services over the target timeframe and meet the security and privacy levels stipulated. The cloud provider can be asked to demonstrate its capabilities and approach to security and privacy enforcement or to undergo an independent evaluation of its installation and systems [All88]. Contacting current clients of the cloud provider's services, either identified independently (e.g., other government agencies) or provided as references by the cloud provider, and assessing their level of satisfaction in areas of security and privacy that are of concern to the organization can also provide insight into the competency of the cloud provider. In addition to evaluating thoroughly the privacy and security levels of the services to be provided, consideration should be given to such items as the following [Len03]:

  - Experience and technical expertise of personnel
  - The vetting process personnel undergo
  - Quality and frequency of security and privacy awareness training provided to personnel
  - Account management practices and accountability
  - The type and effectiveness of the security services provided and underlying mechanisms used
  - The adoption rate of new technologies
  - Change management procedures and processes
  - The cloud provider's track record
  - The ability of the cloud provider to meet the organization's security and privacy policy, procedures, and regulatory compliance needs.

5.3 Initiating and Coincident Activities

The organization has a number of activities to carry out in the second stage of outsourcing, when awarding a contract to a cloud provider and overseeing the terms of the contract throughout its duration.

- **Establish Contractual Obligations.** The organization should ensure that all contractual requirements are explicitly stated in the service agreement, including privacy and security provisions [Gra03, Len03].[25] The agreement should include definitions of both the organization's and the cloud provider's roles and responsibilities. The organization should also make certain that any compensating controls it needs to reduce risk to an

---

[25] For an example of security contract language used in federal procurements, see Security Language for IT Acquisition Efforts, CIO-IT Security-09-48, Revision 1, November 06, 2009 - http://www.gsa.gov/graphics/pbs/CIO_Policy.pdf

acceptable level can be carried out within the terms of the agreement. The terms of the agreement should also include the following items [Gra03]:

- A detailed description of the service environment, including facility locations and applicable security requirements
- Policies, procedures, and standards, including vetting and management of staff
- Predefined service levels and associated costs
- The process for assessing the cloud provider's compliance with the service level agreement, including independent audits and testing
- Specific remedies for harm caused or noncompliance by the cloud provider
- The period of performance and due dates for any deliverable
- The cloud provider's points of interface with the organization
- The organization's responsibilities for providing relevant information and resources to the cloud provider
- Procedures, protections, and restrictions for collocating or commingling organizational data and for handling sensitive data
- The cloud provider's obligations upon contract termination, such as the return and expunging of organizational data.

The previous chapter pointed out additional areas where the organization is especially dependent on the service provider and where the terms of the service agreement should have extreme clarity to avoid potential problems. They include the following items:

- Ownership rights over data
- Locus of organizational data within the cloud environment
- Security and privacy performance visibility
- Service availability and contingency options
- Data backup and recovery
- Incident response coordination and information sharing
- Disaster recovery.

Privacy regulations may be interpreted differently by an organization's legal and privacy officers than by a cloud provider. The organization must take due care when reviewing the controls provided or negotiated in the cloud provider's service agreement to identify and resolve inconsistencies between the organization's and the cloud provider's privacy policies. Organizations must ensure the controls provided are adequate to protect the types of information being planned for deployment to the cloud environment. OMB guidance M-07-16, Safeguarding Against and Responding to the Breach of Personally Identifiable Information, examines the requirements established in the Privacy Act and provides additional guidance regarding an agency's obligations to protect PII.

Before entering into the contract, it is advisable to have an experienced legal advisor review the terms in detail. Non-negotiable service agreements are typically drafted in favor of the cloud provider and may prove to be impracticable for an organization.

Reaching agreement on the terms of service of a negotiated service agreement for public cloud services can be a complicated process fraught with technical and legal issues. If a negotiated service agreement is used, a legal advisor should be involved from the onset to address complicated legal issues that are likely to arise during negotiations.

- **Assess Performance.** Continual assessment of the performance of the cloud provider and quality of the services provisioned is needed to ensure all contract obligations and organizational requirements are being met, and is an essential part of the risk management process.[26] The organization should analyze the state of the system regularly and as frequently as necessary to manage security and privacy risks adequately. Continual assessment allows the organization to take immediate corrective or punitive action for noted deficiencies and also provides a reference point or benchmark for improving the terms of the service agreement [All88, Gra03, Len03].

5.4 Concluding Activities

At the end of a project, when transitioning to another cloud provider, or for other reasons, the organization can decide to enter the final stage of outsourcing and terminate use of the public cloud services and close out the contract. Organizations should perform the following activities preceding the termination of an outsourcing contract:

- **Reaffirm Contractual Obligations.** The organization should alert the cloud provider about any relevant contractual requirements that must be observed upon termination, such as non-disclosure of certain terms of the agreement and sanitization of organizational data from storage media [Len03].

- **Eliminate Physical and Electronic Access Rights.** If any accounts and access rights to an organization's computational resources were assigned to the cloud provider as part of the service agreement, they should be revoked in a timely manner by the organization [All88, Len03]. Similarly, physical access rights of security tokens and badges issued to the cloud provider also need to be revoked, and any personal tokens and badges used for access need to be recovered [All88].

- **Recover Organizational Resources and Data.** The organization should ensure that any resources of the organization made available to the cloud provider under the terms of the service agreement, such as software, equipment, documentation, are returned or recovered in a usable form, as well as any data, programs, scripts, etc. owned by the organization and held by the cloud provider. If the terms of service require the cloud provider to purge data, programs, backup copies, and other cloud consumer content from its environment, evidence such as system reports or logs should be obtained and verified

---

[26] For more information on continuous monitoring and risk management, see SP 800-137, Information Security Continuous Monitoring for Federal Information Systems and Organizations, and SP 800-37 Revision 1, Guide for Applying the Risk Management Framework to Federal Information Systems - http://csrc.nist.gov/publications/index.html.

to ensure that the information has been properly expunged [Len03].[27] These activities should be carried out in compliance with an agency's records management policy.

Having an exit strategy established early in the planning stage, and periodically reviewing and updating its contents, can minimize the problems encountered with the termination of a service agreement, and the effort required to transition applications to another service provider or return them to the organization's data center.

5.5   Summary of Recommendations

Table 3 below summarizes the issues and recommendations that apply at the various stages of outsourcing. They are complementary to those given earlier in Table 1, which stem from specific security and privacy issues.

Table 3: Outsourcing Activities and Recommendations

Areas	Recommendations
Preliminary Activities	Identify security, privacy, and other organizational requirements for cloud services to meet, as a criterion for selecting a cloud provider.
	Analyze the security and privacy controls of a cloud provider's environment and assess the level of risk involved with respect to the control objectives of the organization.
	Evaluate the cloud provider's ability and commitment to deliver cloud services over the target timeframe and meet the security and privacy levels stipulated.
Initiating and Coincident Activities	Ensure that all contractual requirements are explicitly recorded in the service agreement, including privacy and security provisions, and that they are endorsed by the cloud provider.
	Involve a legal advisor in the review of the service agreement and in any negotiations about the terms of service.
	Continually assess the performance of the cloud provider and the quality of the services provisioned to ensure all contract obligations are being met and to manage and mitigate risk.
Concluding Activities	Alert the cloud provider about any contractual requirements that must be observed upon termination.
	Revoke all physical and electronic access rights assigned to the cloud provider and recover physical tokens and badges in a timely manner.
	Ensure that organizational resources made available to or held by the cloud provider under the terms of service agreement are returned or recovered in a usable form, and that information has been properly expunged.

---

[27] For more information on media sanitization, see NIST SP 800-88, Guidelines for Media Sanitization - http://csrc.nist.gov/publications/nistpubs/800-88/NISTSP800-88_rev1.pdf.

6. Conclusion

Cloud computing promises to have far-reaching effects on the systems and networks of federal agencies and other organizations. Emphasis on the cost and performance benefits of public cloud computing should be balanced with the fundamental security and privacy concerns federal agencies and organizations have with these computing environments. Many of the features that make cloud computing attractive can also be at odds with traditional security models and controls. Several critical pieces of technology, such as a solution for federated trust, are not yet fully realized, impinging on successful cloud computing deployments. Determining the security of complex computer systems composed together is also a long-standing security issue that plagues large-scale computing in general, and cloud computing in particular. Attaining high-assurance qualities in system implementations has been an elusive goal of computer security researchers and practitioners and, as demonstrated in the examples given in this report, is also a work in progress for cloud computing. Nevertheless, public cloud computing is a compelling computing paradigm that agencies should consider for their information technology solution set.

Accountability for security and privacy in public cloud deployments cannot be delegated to a cloud provider and remains an obligation for the organization to fulfill. Federal agencies must ensure that any selected public cloud computing solution is configured, deployed, and managed to meet the security, privacy, and other requirements of the organization. Organizational data must be protected in a manner consistent with policies, whether in the organization's computing center or the cloud. The organization must ensure that security and privacy controls are implemented correctly and operate as intended, throughout the system lifecycle.

The transition to an outsourced, public cloud computing environment is in many ways an exercise in risk management. Risk management entails identifying and assessing risk, and taking steps to reduce it to an acceptable level. Assessing and managing risk in cloud computing systems requires continuous monitoring of the security state of the system, and can prove challenging, since significant portions of the computing environment are under the control of the cloud provider and likely beyond the organization's purview. Throughout the system lifecycle, risks that are identified must be carefully balanced against the security and privacy controls available and the expected benefits from their utilization. Too many controls can be inefficient and ineffective. Federal agencies and other organizations must work diligently to maintain an appropriate balance between the number and strength of controls and the risks associated with cloud computing solutions.

Cloud computing is a new computing paradigm that is still emerging. Technology advances are expected to improve performance and other qualities of services from public clouds, including privacy and security. Many agency systems are long lived and, if transitioned to a public cloud, will likely experience technology and other changes over the course of their lifetime. Cloud providers may decide to sell or merge their offerings with other companies; service offerings may be eclipsed by those of another cloud provider or fall into disfavor; and organizations may be required to re-compete an existing contract for cloud services, when all option years have been exhausted. Eventually having to displace some systems to another public cloud is a distinct possibility that federal agencies and other organizations must not overlook.

7. References

[All88]   Julia Allen et al., Security for Information Technology Service Contracts, CMU/SEI-SIM-003, Software Engineering Institute, Carnegie Mellon University, January 1988, <URL: http://www.sei.cmu.edu/reports/98sim003.pdf>.

[Alp11]   Pavel Alpeyev, Joseph Galante, Mariko Yasu, Amazon.com Server Said to Have Been Used in Sony Attack, Bloomberg, May 14, 2011, <URL: http://www.bloomberg.com/news/2011-05-13/sony-network-said-to-have-been-invaded-by-hackers-using-amazon-com-server.html>.

[And11]   Nate Anderson, Anonymous vs. HBGary: the Aftermath, Ars Technica, February 24, 2011, <URL: http://arstechnica.com/tech-policy/news/2011/02/anonymous-vs-hbgary-the-aftermath.ars>.

[Arm10]   Michael Armbrust et al., A View of Cloud Computing, Communications of the ACM, Association for Computing Machinery, Vol. 53, No. 4, April 2010.

[Ash10]   Warwick Ashford, Google Confirms Dismissal of Engineer for Breaching Privacy Rules, Computer Weekly, September 16, 2010, <URL: http://www.computerweekly.com/Articles/2010/09/16/242877/Google-confirms-dismissal-of-engineer-for-breaching-privacy.htm>.

[Avo00]   Frederick M. Avolio, Best Practices in Network Security, Network Computing, March 20, 2000, <URL: http://www.networkcomputing.com/1105/1105f2.html>.

[Bar05]   Elaine B. Barker, William C. Barker, Annabelle Lee, Guideline for Implementing Cryptography In the Federal Government, NIST Special Publication 800-21, Second Edition, December 2005, <URL: http://csrc.nist.gov/publications/nistpubs/800-21-1/sp800-21-1_Dec2005.pdf>.

[Bin09]   David Binning, Top Five Cloud Computing Security Issues, Computer Weekly, April 24, 2009, <URL: http://www.computerweekly.com/Articles/2010/01/12/235782/Top-five-cloud-computing-security-issues.htm>.

[Bos11]   Bianca Bosker, Dropbox Bug Made Passwords Unnecessary, Left Data At Risk For Hours, The Huffington Post, June 21, 2011, <URL: http://www.huffingtonpost.com/2011/06/21/dropbox-security-bug-passwords_n_881085.html>.

[Bra10]   Simon Bradshaw, Christopher Millard, Ian Walden, Contracts for Clouds: Comparison and Analysis of the Terms and Conditions of Cloud Computing Services, Queen Mary School of Law Legal Studies, Research Paper No. 63/2010, September 2, 2010, <URL: http://papers.ssrn.com/sol3/papers.cfm?abstract_id=1662374>.

[Bra11] Tony Bradley, Google, Skype, Yahoo Targeted by Rogue Comodo SSL Certificates, PCWorld, March 23, 2011, <URL: http://www.pcworld.com/businesscenter/article/223147/google_skype_yahoo_targeted_by_rogue_comodo_ssl_certificates.html>.

[Bro08] Jon Brodkin, Loss of Customer Data Spurs Closure of Online Storage Service 'The Linkup,' Network World, August 11, 2008, <URL: http://www.networkworld.com/news/2008/081108-linkup-failure.html?page=1>.

[Bro09] Carl Brooks, Amazon EC2 Attack Prompts Customer Support Changes, Tech Target, October 12, 2009, <URL: http://searchcloudcomputing.techtarget.com/news/article/0,289142,sid201_gci1371090,00.html>.

[Cal09] Michael Calore, Ma.gnolia Suffers Major Data Loss, Site Taken Offline, Wired Magazine, January 30, 2009, <URL: http://www.wired.com/epicenter/2009/01/magnolia-suffer/>.

[CAO09] Report from Office of the City Administrative Officer: Analysis of Proposed Contract, City of Los Angeles, CAO File No.:0150-00813-0001, July 9, 2009, <URL: http://clkrep.lacity.org/onlinedocs/2009/09-1714_rpt_cao_7-9-09.pdf>.

[Cap09] Dawn Cappelli, Andrew Moore, Randall Trzeciak, Timothy J. Shimeall, Common Sense Guide to Prevention and Detection of Insider Threats, Third Edition, Version 3.1, CERT, January 2009, <URL: http://www.cert.org/archive/pdf/CSG-V3.pdf>.

[CBC04] USA Patriot Act Comes under Fire in B.C. Report, CBC News, October 30, 2004, <URL: http://www.cbc.ca/canada/story/2004/10/29/patriotact_bc041029.html>.

[Cha10] Rajarshi Chakraborty, Srilakshmi Ramireddy, T.S. Raghu, H. Raghav Rao, The Information Assurance Practices of Cloud Computing Vendors, IEEE IT Pro, Vol. 12, Issue 4, July/August 2010.

[Cho09] Richard Chow et al., Controlling Data in the Cloud: Outsourcing Computation without Outsourcing Control, ACM Workshop on Cloud Computing Security, Chicago, Illinois, November 2009, <URL: http://www2.parc.com/csl/members/eshi/docs/ccsw.pdf>.

[CIO10a] Privacy Recommendations for the Use of Cloud Computing by Federal Departments and Agencies, CIO Council, Privacy Committee, Web 2.0/Cloud Computing Subcommittee, August 2010, <URL: http://www.cio.gov/Documents/Privacy-Recommendations-Cloud-Computing-8-19-2010.docx>.

[CIO10b]   Federal Enterprise Architecture Security and Privacy Profile, Version 3, September 30, 2010, <URL: http://www.cio.gov/Documents/FEA-Security-Privacy-Profile-v3-09-30-2010.pdf>.

[Cla09]   Gavin Clarke, Microsoft's Azure Cloud Suffers First Crash, The Register, March 16, 2009, <URL: http://www.theregister.co.uk/2009/03/16/azure_cloud_crash/>.

[CLA10]   Second Status Report on the Implementation of the Google E-Mail and Collaboration System, City Administrative Officer, City of Los Angeles, July 9, 2010, <URL: http://clkrep.lacity.org/onlinedocs/2009/09-1714_rpt_cao_7-9-10.pdf>.

[CLA11a]   Second Amendment to Contract Number C-116359 between the City and Computer Sciences Corporation for E-Mail and Collaboration Solution (Google), Inter-Departmental Correspondence, City of Los Angeles, December 9, 2011, <URL: http://clkrep.lacity.org/onlinedocs/2009/09-1714-S2_RPT_CLA_12-09-11.pdf>.

[CLA11b]   Record of Council Action Regarding Second Amendment to Contract Number C-116359, City of Los Angeles, December 20, 2011, <URL: http://clkrep.lacity.org/onlinedocs/2009/09-1714-S2_CA_12-14-11.pdf>.

[Coc97]   Steve Cocheo, The Bank Robber, the Quote, and the Final Irony, nFront, American Bankers Association (ABA) Banking Journal, 1997, <URL: http://www.banking.com/aba/profile_0397.htm>.

[Cou09]   David A. Couillard, Defogging the Cloud: Applying Fourth Amendment Principles to Evolving Privacy Expectations in Cloud Computing, Minnesota Law Review, Vol. 93, No. 6, June 2009.

[Cra08]   George Craciun, Amazon EC2 Spreads Malware, Softpedia, July 1, 2008, <URL: http://news.softpedia.com/news/Amazon-EC2-Spreads-Malware-89014.shtml>.

[Cra10]   Personal conversation with Kevin K. Crawford, Assistant General Manager, Information Technology Agency, City of Los Angeles, December 15, 2010.

[Cra11]   Personal conversation with Kevin K. Crawford, Assistant General Manager, Information Technology Agency, City of Los Angeles, August 22, 2011.

[CSA11a]   Encryption and Key Management, Cloud Security Alliance, January 12, 2011, <URL: https://wiki.cloudsecurityalliance.org/guidance/index.php/Encryption_and_Key_Management>.

[CSA11b]   Cloud Controls Matrix, Version 1.2, Cloud Security Alliance, August 26, 2011, <URL: https://cloudsecurityalliance.org/wp-content/uploads/2011/08/CSA_CCM_v1.2.xls>.

[CSC10]   LA SECS Overview: SaaS E-mail and Collaboration Solution (SECS) – Implementing Google for the Los Angeles, CSC, April 15, 2010, <URL: http://assets1.csc.com/lef/downloads/LEFBriefing_CSC_LA_Google_041510.pdf>.

[CWD10]   Notice of Deficiencies-CSC Contract No. C-116359, City of Los Angeles, December 9, 2010, <URL: http://www.consumerwatchdog.org/resources/googdeficiency.pdf>.

[Daw05]   Alistair B. Dawson, Understanding Electronic Discovery and Solving Its Problems, 56th Annual Program on Oil and Gas Law, The Center for American and International Law, February 17-18, 2005, Houston, Texas, <URL: http://www.brsfirm.com/publications/docs/00037W.pdf>.

[Dem10]   Kelley Dempsey et al., Information Security Continuous Monitoring for Federal Information Systems and Organizations, Initial Public Draft, SP 800-137, NIST, September 2011, <URL: http://csrc.nist.gov/publications/nistpubs/800-137/SP800-137-Final.pdf>.

[Dig08]   Larry Dignam, Amazon Explains Its S3 Outage, ZDNET, February 16, 2008, <URL: http://www.zdnet.com/blog/btl/amazon-explains-its-s3-outage/8010>.

[Dij10]   Marten van Dijk, Ari Juels, On the Impossibility of Cryptography Alone for Privacy-Preserving Cloud Computing, 5th USENIX Workshop on Hot Topics in Security (HotSec '10), August 10, 2010, <URL: http://www.usenix.org/event/hotsec10/tech/full_papers/vanDijk.pdf>

[Din10]   Jocelyn Ding, LA's Move to Google Apps Continues Apace, Official Google Enterprise Blog, August 04, 2010, <URL: http://googleenterprise.blogspot.com/2010/08/las-move-to-google-apps-continues-apace.html>.

[DoC00]   Safe Harbor Privacy Principles, U.S. Department of Commerce, July 21, 2000, <URL: http://export.gov/safeharbor/eu/eg_main_018475.asp>.

[DPW10]   LA DPW Engineering Newsletter, No. 10-22, Los Angeles City, Department of Public Works (DPW), April 21, 2010, <URL: http://eng.lacity.org/newsletters/2010/04-21-10.pdf>.

[Dun10a] John E. Dunn, Ultra-secure Firefox Offered to UK Bank Users, Techworld, February 26, 2010, <URL: http://news.techworld.com/security/3213740/ultra-secure-firefox-offered-to-uk-bank-users/>.

[Dun10b] John E. Dunn, Virtualised USB Key Beats Keyloggers, Techworld, February 22, 2010, <URL: http://news.techworld.com/security/3213277/virtualised-usb-key-beats-keyloggers/>.

[DVA]   What the VA Is Doing to Protect Your Privacy, VA Pamphlet 005-06-1, Department of Veteran Affairs, <URL: http://www.privacy.va.gov/docs/VA005-06-1_privacy_brochure.pdf>.

[Eis05]   Margaret P. Eisenhauer, Privacy and Security Law Issues in Off-shore Outsourcing Transactions, Hunton & Williams LLP, The Outsourcing Institute, Legal Corner, February 15, 2005, <URL: http://www.outsourcing.com/legal_corner/pdf/Outsourcing_Privacy.pdf>.

[Fer07]   Peter Ferrie, Attacks on Virtual Machine Emulators, White Paper, Symantec Corporation, January 2007, <URL: http://www.symantec.com/avcenter/reference/Virtual_Machine_Threats.pdf>.

[Fer09]   Tim Ferguson, Salesforce.com Outage Hits Thousands of Businesses, CNET News, January 8, 2009, <URL: http://news.cnet.com/8301-1001_3-10136540-92.html>.

[Fer10]   David S. Ferreiro, Guidance on Managing Records in Cloud Computing Environments, NARA Bulletin 2010-05, September 8, 2010, <URL: http://www.archives.gov:80/records-mgmt/bulletins/2010/2010-05.html>.

[Fre08]   Stefan Frei, Thomas Duebendorfer, Gunter Ollmann, Martin May, Understanding the Web Browser Threat: Examination of vulnerable online Web browser populations and the "insecurity iceberg", ETH Zurich, Tech Report Nr. 288, 2008, <URL: http://e-collection.ethbib.ethz.ch/eserv/eth:30892/eth-30892-01.pdf>.

[Fow09]   Geoffrey Fowler, Ben Worthen, The Internet Industry Is on a Cloud – Whatever That May Mean, The Wall Street Journal, March 26, 2009, <URL: http://online.wsj.com/article/SB123802623665542725.html>.

[FTC07]   Fair Information Practice Principles, Federal Trade Commission, June 25, 2007, <URL: http://www.ftc.gov/reports/privacy3/fairinfo.shtm>.

[Gaj09]   Sebastian Gajek, Meiko Jensen, Lijun Liao, and Jörg Schwenk, Analysis of Signature Wrapping Attacks and Countermeasures, IEEE International Conference on Web Services, Los Angeles, California, July 2009.

[Gar05]   Tal Garfinkel, Mendel Rosenblum, When Virtual Is Harder than Real: Security Challenges in Virtual Machine Based Computing Environments, HotOS'05, Santa Fe, New Mexico, June 2005, <URL: http://www.stanford.edu/~talg/papers/HOTOS05/virtual-harder-hotos05.pdf>.

[Gar07]   Simson Garfinkel, An Evaluation of Amazon's Grid Computing Services: EC2, S3 and SQS, Technical Report TR-08-07, Center for Research on Computation and Society, School for Engineering and Applied Sciences, Harvard University, July 2007, <URL: http://simson.net/clips/academic/2007.Harvard.S3.pdf>.

[GAO06] Privacy: Domestic and Offshore Outsourcing of Personal Information in Medicare, Medicaid, and TRICARE, United States Government Accountability Office, GAO-06-676, September 2006, <URL: http://www.gao.gov/new.items/d06676.pdf>.

[GAO10] Contractor Integrity: Stronger Safeguards Needed for Contractor Access to Sensitive Information, United States Government Accountability Office, GAO-10-693, September 2010, <URL: http://www.gao.gov/new.items/d10693.pdf>.

[Gee08] Daniel E. Geer, Complexity Is the Enemy, IEEE Security and Privacy, Vol. 6, No. 6, November/December 2008.

[Gon09] Reyes Gonzalez, Jose Gasco, and Juan Llopis, Information Systems Outsourcing Reasons and Risks: An Empirical Study, International Journal of Human and Social Sciences, Vol. 4, No. 3, 2009, <URL: http://www.waset.org/journals/ijhss/v4/v4-3-24.pdf>.

[Goo09a] Dan Goodin, Salesforce.com Outage Exposes Cloud's Dark Linings, The Register, January 6, 2009, <URL: http://www.theregister.co.uk/2009/01/06/salesforce_outage/>.

[Goo09b] Dan Goodin, Webhost Hack Wipes Out Data for 100,000 Sites, The Register, June 8, 2009, <URL: http://www.theregister.co.uk/2009/06/08/webhost_attack/>.

[Goo10] Dan Goodin, Privacy Watchdog Pack Demands Facebook Close the 'App Gap', The Register, June 16, 2010, <URL: http://www.theregister.co.uk/2010/06/16/facebook_privacy/>.

[Gou11] Jeff Gould, Los Angeles Ends Google Apps for LAPD; Decision Bigger Than You Think, AOL Government, December 19, 2011, <URL: http://gov.aol.com/2011/12/19/los-angeles-ends-google-apps-for-lapd-decision-bigger-than-you/>.

[Gra03] Tim Grance et al., Guide to Information Technology Security Services, Special Publication 800-35, National Institute of Standards and Technology, October 2003, <URL: http://csrc.nist.gov/publications/nistpubs/800-35/NIST-SP800-35.pdf>.

[Gre09] Andy Greenberg, IBM's Blindfolded Calculator, Forbes Magazine, July 13, 2009, <URL: http://www.forbes.com/forbes/2009/0713/breakthroughs-privacy-super-secret-encryption.html>.

[Gro10] Bernd Grobauer, Thomas Schreck, Towards Incident Handling in the Cloud: Challenges and Approaches, ACM Cloud Computing Security Workshop, Chicago, Illinois, October 8, 2010.

[Gru09]   Nils Gruschka, Luigi Lo Iacono, Vulnerable Cloud: SOAP Message Security Validation Revisited, IEEE International Conference on Web Services, Los Angeles, California, July 2009.

[Gun08]   Mike Gunderloy, Who Protects Your Cloud Data?, Web Worker Daily, January 13, 2008, <URL: http://webworkerdaily.com/2008/01/13/who-protects-your-cloud-data/>.

[Han06]   Saul Hansell, Online Trail Can Lead To Court, The New York Times, February 4, 2006,   <URL: http://query.nytimes.com/gst/fullpage.html?res=9B03E5D7163EF937A35751C0A96 09C8B63>.

[HR2458] Federal Information Security Management Act of 2002 (FISMA), H.R. 2458, Title III—Information Security, <URL: http://csrc.nist.gov/drivers/documents/FISMA-final.pdf>.

[Inf09]   Twitter Email Account Hack Highlights Cloud Dangers, Infosecurity Magazine, July 23, 2009, <URL: http://www.infosecurity-magazine.com/view/2668/twitter-email-account-hack-highlights-cloud-dangers-/>.

[Jac07]   Dean Jacobs, Stefan Aulbach, Ruminations on Multi-Tenant Databases, Fachtagung für Datenbanksysteme in Business, Technologie und Web, Aachen, Germany, March 5-9, 2007, <URL: http://www.btw2007.de/paper/p514.pdf>.

[Jan08]   Wayne Jansen, Karen Scarfone, Guidelines on Cell Phone and PDA Security, Special Publication (SP) 800-124, National Institute of Standards and Technology, October 2008, <URL: http://csrc.nist.gov/publications/nistpubs/800-124/SP800-124.pdf>

[Jen09]   Meiko Jensen, Jörg Schwenk, Nils Gruschka, Luigi Lo Iacono, On Technical Security Issues in Cloud Computing, IEEE International Conference on Cloud Computing, Bangalore, India, September 21-25, 2009.

[JTF10]   Guide for Applying the Risk Management Framework to Federal Information Systems: A Security Life Cycle Approach, Joint Task Force Transformation Initiative, NIST Special Publication 800-37, Revision 1, <URL: http://csrc.nist.gov/publications/nistpubs/800-37-rev1/sp800-37-rev1-final.pdf>.

[Kan09]   Balachandra Reddy Kandukuri, Ramakrishna Paturi V, Atanu Rakshit, Cloud Security Issues, IEEE International Conference on Services Computing, Bangalore, India, September 21-25, 2009.

[Kar08]   Paul A. Karger, I/O for Virtual Machine Monitors: Security and Performance Issues, IEEE Security and Privacy, September/October 2008.

[Kat10] Neil Katz, Austin Plane Crash: Pilot Joseph Andrew Stack May Have Targeted IRS Offices, Says FBI, CBS News, February 18, 2010, <URL: http://www.cbsnews.com/8301-504083_162-6220271-504083.html?tag=contentMain%3bcontentBody>.

[Kel05] Yared Keleta, J.H.P. Eloff, H.S. Venter, Proposing a Secure XACML Architecture Ensuring Privacy and Trust, Research in Progress Paper, University of Pretoria, 2005, <URL: http://icsa.cs.up.ac.za/issa/2005/Proceedings/Research/093_Article.pdf>.

[Ker10] Sean Michael Kerner, Mozilla Confirms Security Threat from Malicious Firefox Add-ons, eSecurity Planet, February 5, 2010, <URL: http://www.esecurityplanet.com/news/article.php/3863331/Mozilla-Confirms-Security-Threat-From-Malicious-Firefox-Add-Ons.htm>.

[Ker11] Justin Kern, Amazon Apologizes, Cites Human Error in Cloud Interruption, Information Management Online, April 29, 2011, <URL: http://www.information-management.com/news/cloud_SaaS_data_center_downtime_storage_Amazon-10020215-1.html>.

[Kin06] Samuel King, Peter Chen, Yi-Min Wang, Chad Verbowski, Helen Wang, Jacob Lorch, SubVirt: Implementing Malware with Virtual Machines, IEEE Symposium on Security and Privacy, Berkeley, California, May 2006, <URL: http://www.eecs.umich.edu/~pmchen/papers/king06.pdf>.

[Kre07] Brian Krebs, Salesforce.com Acknowledges Data Loss, Security Fix, The Washington Post, November 6, 2007, <URL: http://blog.washingtonpost.com/securityfix/2007/11/salesforcecom_acknowledges_dat.html>.

[Kre08] Brian Krebs, Amazon: Hey Spammers, Get Off My Cloud! The Washington Post, July 1, 2008, <URL: http://voices.washingtonpost.com/securityfix/2008/07/amazon_hey_spammers_get_off_my.html>.

[Kow08] Eileen Kowalski et al., Insider Threat Study: Illicit Cyber Activity in the Government Sector, U.S. Secret Service and Carnegie Mellon University, Software Engineering Institute, January 2008, <URL: http://www.cert.org/archive/pdf/insiderthreat_gov2008.pdf>.

[Kri08] Michael Krigsma, Amazon S3 Web Services Down. Bad, Bad News for Customers, ZDNET, February 15, 2008, <URL: http://blogs.zdnet.com/projectfailures/?p=602>.

[Kum08] Sushil Kumar, Oracle Database Backup in the Cloud, White Paper, Oracle Corporation, September 2008.

[Lab95]   Stephen Labaton, 2 Men Held in Attempt to Bomb I.R.S. Office, New York Times, December 29, 1995, <URL: http://www.nytimes.com/1995/12/29/us/2-men-held-in-attempt-to-bomb-irs-office.html?pagewanted=1>.

[LAPD10] Supplemental Report to the City Administrative Officer: Second Status Report on the Implementation of the Google E-Mail and Collaboration System (C.F. 09-1714), Los Angeles Police Department, City of Los Angeles, <URL: http://clkrep.lacity.org/onlinedocs/2009/09-1714_rpt_lapd_7-8-10.pdf>.

[Lat96]   20-Year Term in Plot to Bomb IRS Offices, Nation In Brief, Los Angeles Times, August 10, 1996, <URL: http://articles.latimes.com/1996-08-10/news/mn-32970_1_20-year-term>.

[Lea09]   Neal Leavitt, Is Cloud Computing Really Ready for Prime Time?, IEEE Computer, January 2009.

[Len03]   Bee Leng, A Security Guide for Acquiring Outsourced Service, GIAC GSEC Practical (v1.4b), SANS Institute, August 19, 2003, <URL: http://www.sans.org/reading_room/whitepapers/services/a_security_guide_for_acquiring_outsourced_service_1241>.

[Mag10]   James Maguire, How Cloud Computing Security Resembles the Financial Meltdown, Datamation, internet.com, April 27, 2010, <URL: http://itmanagement.earthweb.com/netsys/article.php/3878811/How-Cloud-Computing-Security-Resembles-the-Financial-Meltdown.htm>.

[Mcc10]   Erika McCallister, Tim Grance, Karen Scarfone, Guide to Protecting the Confidentiality of Personally Identifiable Information (PII), SP 800-122, National Institute of Standards and Technology, April 2010, <URL: http://csrc.nist.gov/publications/nistpubs/800-122/sp800-122.pdf>.

[Mcd10]   Steve McDonald, Legal and Quasi-Legal Issues in Cloud Computing Contracts, Workshop Document, EDUCAUSE and NACUBO Workshop on Cloud Computing and Shared Services, Tempe, Arizona, February 8–10, 2010, <URL: http://net.educause.edu/section_params/conf/CCW10/issues.pdf>.

[Mcm07] Robert McMillan, Salesforce.com Warns Customers of Phishing Scam, PC Magazine, IDG News Network, November 6, 2007, <URL: http://www.pcworld.com/businesscenter/article/139353/salesforcecom_warns_customers_of_phishing_scam.html>.

[Mcm09a] Robert McMillan, Hackers Find a Home in Amazon's EC2 Cloud, Infoworld, IDG News Network, December 10, 2009, <URL: http://www.infoworld.com/d/cloud-computing/hackers-find-home-in-amazons-ec2-cloud-742>.

[Mcm09b] Robert McMillan, Misdirected Spyware Infects Ohio Hospital, PC Magazine, IDG News Service September 17, 2009, <URL: http://www.pcworld.com/businesscenter/article/172185/misdirected_spyware_infects _ohio_hospital.html>.

[Mee09] Haroon Meer, Nick Arvanitis, Marco Slaviero, Clobbering the Cloud, Part 4 of 5, Black Hat USA Talk Write-up, SensePost SDH Labs, 2009, <URL: http://www.sensepost.com/labs/conferences/clobbering_the_cloud/amazon>.

[Mel11] Peter Mell, Tim Grance, The NIST Definition of Cloud Computing, Special Publication 800-145, National Institute of Standards and Technology, August 2011, <URL: http://csrc.nist.gov/publications/nistpubs/800-145/sp800-145.pdf>.

[Met09] Cade Metz, DDoS Attack Rains Down on Amazon Cloud, The Register, October 5, 2009, <URL: http://www.theregister.co.uk/2009/10/05/amazon_bitbucket_outage/>.

[Met11] Cade Metz, Amazon Cloud Fell from Sky after Botched Network Upgrade, The Register, April 29, 2011, <URL: http://www.theregister.co.uk/2011/04/29/amazon_ec2_outage_post_mortem/>.

[Mic09] The Windows Azure Malfunction This Weekend, Windows Azure <Team Blog>, Microsoft Corporation, March 18, 2009, <URL: http://blogs.msdn.com/windowsazure/archive/2009/03/18/the-windows-azure-malfunction-this-weekend.aspx>.

[Mic10] Fact-Based Comparison of Hosted Services: Google vs. Microsoft, Microsoft Corporation, May 16, 2010, <URL: http://download.microsoft.com/download/0/5/F/05FF69ED-6F8F-4357-863B-12E27D6F1115/Hosted%20Services%20Comparison%20Whitepaper%20-%20Google%20vs%20Microsoft.pdf>.

[Mil08] Rich Miller, Major Outage for Amazon S3 and EC2, Data Center Knowledge, February 15, 2008, <URL: http://www.datacenterknowledge.com/archives/2008/02/15/major-outage-for-amazon-s3-and-ec2/>.

[Mil09] Rich Miller, Lightning Strike Triggers Amazon EC2 Outage, Data Center Knowledge, June 11, 2009, <URL: http://www.datacenterknowledge.com/archives/2009/06/11/lightning-strike-triggers-amazon-ec2-outage/>.

[Mod08] Austin Modine, Downed Salesforce Systems Slow Europe and US, The Register, February 11, 2008, <URL: http://www.theregister.co.uk/2008/02/11/salesforce_outages_feb_2008/>.

[MRG10] Online Banking: Browser Security Project, Malware Research Group, Zorin Nexus Ltd., June 2010, <URL: http://malwareresearchgroup.com/wp-content/uploads/2009/01/Online-Banking-Browser-Security-Project-June-201013.zip>.

[Mul10] Robert Mullins, The Biggest Cloud on the Planet is Owned by the Crooks, Network World, March 22, 2010, <URL: http://www.networkworld.com/community/node/58829>.

[Nav10] Eliminating the Data Security and Regulatory Concerns of Using SaaS Applications, White Paper, Navajo Systems, January 2010, <URL: http://www.navajosystems.com/media/Virtual_Private_SaaS_White_Paper.pdf>.

[Obe08a] Jon Oberheide, Evan Cooke, Farnam Jahanian, Empirical Exploitation of Live Virtual Machine Migration, Black Hat Security Conference, Washington, DC, February 2008, <URL: http://www.blackhat.com/presentations/bh-dc-08/Oberheide/Whitepaper/bh-dc-08-oberheide-WP.pdf>.

[Obe08b] Jon Oberheide, Evan Cooke, Farnam Jahanian, CloudAV: N-Version Antivirus in the Network Cloud, USENIX Security Symposium, Association, San Jose, CA, July 28-August 1, 2008, <URL: http://www.eecs.umich.edu/fjgroup/pubs/usenix08-cloudav.pdf>.

[OECD80] OECD Guidelines on the Protection of Privacy and Transborder Flows of Personal Data, Organisation for Economic Co-operation and Development, September 23,1980, <URL: http://www.oecd.org/document/18/0,3746,en_2649_34255_1815186_1_1_1_1,00.html>.

[Opp03] David Oppenheimer, Archana Ganapathi, David Patterson, Why Do Internet Services Fail, and What Can Be Done About It?, 4th USENIX Symposium on Internet Technologies and Systems, March 2003, <URL: http://roc.cs.berkeley.edu/papers/usits03.pdf>.

[Orm07] Tavis Ormandy, An Empirical Study into the Security Exposure to Hosts of Hostile Virtualized Environments, 2007, <URL: http://taviso.decsystem.org/virtsec.pdf>.

[Ove10] Stephanie Overby, How to Negotiate a Better Cloud Computing Contract, CIO, April 21, 2010, <URL: http://www.cio.com/article/591629/How_to_Negotiate_a_Better_Cloud_Computing_Contract>.

[Owa10] Cloud-10 Multi Tenancy and Physical Security, The Open Web Application Security Project, Cloud Top 10 Security Risks, August 30, 2010, <URL: https://www.owasp.org/index.php/Cloud-10_Multi_Tenancy_and_Physical_Security>.

[Pea09]   Siani Pearson, Taking Account of Privacy When Designing Cloud Computing Services, International Conference on Software Engineering (ICSE) Workshop on Software Engineering Challenges of Cloud Computing, Vancouver, Canada, May 23, 2009.

[Pep11a]   Julianne Pepitone, Amazon EC2 Outage Downs Reddit, Quora, CNN Money, April 22, 2011, <URL: http://money.cnn.com/2011/04/21/technology/amazon_server_outage/index.htm>.

[Pep11b]   Julianne Pepitone, RSA Offers to Replace All SecurID Tokens after Hack Attack, CNN Money Tech, June 8, 2011, <URL: http://money.cnn.com/2011/06/08/technology/securid_hack/index.htm>.

[Per11]   By Juan Carlos Perez, Microsoft's Cloud BPOS Suite Suffers Outage Again, InfoWorld Inc., June 22, 2011, <URL: http://www.infoworld.com/d/applications/microsofts-cloud-bpos-suite-suffers-outage-again-050>.

[Pon10]   Larry Ponemon, Security of Cloud Computing Users, Ponemon Institute, May 12, 2010, <URL: http://www.ca.com/files/IndustryResearch/security-cloud-computing-users_235659.pdf>.

[Pro07]   Niels Provos, Dean McNamee, Panayiotis Mavrommatis, Ke Wang, Nagendra Modadugu, The Ghost in the Browser: Analysis of Web-based Malware, Hot Topics in Understanding Botnets (HotBots), April 10, 2007, Cambridge, Massachusetts, <URL: http://www.usenix.org/events/hotbots07/tech/full_papers/provos/provos.pdf>.

[Pro09]   Niels Provos, Moheeb Abu Rajab, Panayiotis Mavrommatis, Cybercrime 2.0: When the Cloud Turns Dark, Communications of the ACM, April 2009.

[Pro10]   Cloud Security and Privacy: Data Security and Storage, November 18, 2010, <URL http://mscerts.programming4.us/programming/Cloud%20Security%20and%20Privacy%20%20%20Data%20Security%20and%20Storage.aspx>.

[Rag09]   Steve Ragan, New Service Offers Cloud Cracking for WPA, The Tech Herald, December 8, 2009, <URL: http://www.thetechherald.com/article.php/200950/4906/New-service-offers-cloud-cracking-for-WPA>.

[Rap09]   J.R. Raphael, Facebook Privacy Change Sparks Federal Complaint, PC World, February 17, 2009, <URL: http://www.pcworld.com/article/159703/facebook.html?tk=rel_news>.

[Ref10]   Security Within a Virtualized Environment: A New Layer in Layered Security, White Paper, Reflex Security, retrieved April 23, 2010, <URL:

http://www.vmware.com/files/pdf/partners/security/security-virtualized-whitepaper.pdf>.

[Ris09]   Thomas Ristenpart, Eran Tromer, Hovav Shacham, Stefan Savage, Hey, You, Get Off of My Cloud: Exploring Information Leakage in Third-Party Compute Clouds, ACM Conference on Computer and Communications Security, November 2009, <URL: http://cseweb.ucsd.edu/~hovav/dist/cloudsec.pdf>.

[Row07]   Brent R. Rowe, Will Outsourcing IT Security Lead to a Higher Social Level of Security?, Research Triangle Institute International, July 2007, <URL: http://weis2007.econinfosec.org/papers/47.pdf>.

[Sar10]   David Sarno, Los Angeles Police Department Switch to Google E-mail System Hits Federal Roadblock, Los Angeles Times, November 03, 2010, <URL: http://articles.latimes.com/2010/nov/03/business/la-fi-google-la-20101103>.

[Sar11a]   David Sarno, Google Facing Hurdles in Bid to Provide Email Service to Governments, Los Angeles Times, April 14, 2011, <URL: http://articles.latimes.com/2011/apr/14/business/la-fi-google-email-20110414>.

[Sar11b]   David Sarno, L.A. won't put LAPD on Google's cloud-based email system, Los Angeles Times, December 14, 2011, <URL: http://articles.latimes.com/2011/dec/14/business/la-fi-google-email-20111215>.

[Sca11]   Karen Scarfone, Murugiah Souppaya, Paul Hoffman, Guide to Security for Full Virtualization Technologies, Special Publication 800-125, National Institute of Standards and Technology, January 2011, <URL: http://csrc.nist.gov/publications/nistpubs/800-125/SP800-125-final.pdf >.

[Sch00]   Bruce Schneier, Crypto-Gram Newsletter, Software Complexity and Security, March 15, 2000, <URL: http://www.schneier.com/crypto-gram-0003.html#8>.

[Sch10]   Jeff Schnepper, Don't Like the Tax Law? Don't Shoot the IRS, MSN, March 10, 2010,   <URL: http://articles.moneycentral.msn.com/Taxes/blog/page.aspx?post=1692029&_blg=1,1619827>.

[Sch11]   Mathew J. Schwartz, Are You Ready for an FBI Server Takedown?, Information Week, July 01, 2011, <URL: http://www.informationweek.com/news/security/management/231000897>.

[Sha08]   Amit Shah, Kernel-based Virtualization with KVM, Linux Magazine, issue 86, January 2008, <URL: http://www.linux-magazine.com/w3/issue/86/Kernel_Based_Virtualization_With_KVM.pdf>.

[Sec05]   VMware Vulnerability in NAT Networking, BugTraq, SecurityFocus, December 21, 2005, <URL: http://www.securityfocus.com/archive/1/420017 and http://www.securityfocus.com/bid/15998/>.

[SECS09]   Professional Services Contract, SAAS E-Mail & Collaboration Solution (SECS), City of Los Angeles, November 10, 2009, <URL: https://sites.google.com/a/lageecs.lacity.org/la-geecs-blog/home/faqs-1/C-116359_c_11-20-09.pdf?attredirects=0&d=1>

[She05]   Tim Shelton, Remote Heap Overflow, ACSSEC-2005-11-25 - 0x1, <URL: http://packetstormsecurity.org/0512-advisories/ACSSEC-2005-11-25-0x1.txt>.

[Sla09]   Marco Slaviero, BlackHat Presentation Demo Vids: Amazon, part 4 of 5, AMIBomb, August 8, 2009, <URL: http://www.sensepost.com/blog/3797.html>.

[Sob06]   Charles H. Sobey, Laslo Orto, and Glenn Sakaguchi, Drive-Independent Data-Recovery: The Current State-of-the-Art, IEEE Transactions on Magnetics, February 2006, <URL: http://www.actionfront.com/whitepaper/Drive%20Independent%20Data%20Recovery%20TMRC2005%20Preprint.pdf>.

[Som11]   Juraj Somorovsky et al., All Your Clouds Belong to Us – Security Analysis of Cloud Management Interfaces, ACM Cloud Computing Security Workshop (CCSW), Chicago, October 21, 2011.

[Sto02]   Gary Stoneburner, Alice Goguen, and Alexis Feringa, Risk Management Guide for Information Technology Systems, SP 800-30, NIST, July 2002, <URL: http://csrc.nist.gov/publications/nistpubs/800-30/sp800-30.pdf>.

[Sto10]   Jon Stokes, EMC's Atmos Shutdown Shows Why Cloud Lock-in is Still Scary, Ars Technica, July 2010, <URL: http://arstechnica.com/business/news/2010/07/emcs-atmos-shutdown-shows-why-cloud-lock-in-is-still-scary.ars>.

[Sut09]   John D. Sutter, Twitter Hack Raises Questions about 'Cloud Computing', CNN, July 16, 2009, <URL: http://edition.cnn.com/2009/TECH/07/16/twitter.hack/>.

[Swa06]   Marianne Swanson, Joan Hash, Pauline Bowen, Guide for Developing Security Plans for Federal Information Systems, NIST, Special Publication 800-18, Revision 1, February 2006, <URL: http://csrc.nist.gov/publications/nistpubs/800-18-Rev1/sp800-18-Rev1-final.pdf>.

[UCG10]   Cloud Computing Use Cases White Paper, Version 4.0, Cloud Computing Use Case Discussion Group, July 2, 2010, <URL: http://opencloudmanifesto.org/Cloud_Computing_Use_Cases_Whitepaper-4_0.pdf>.

[Val08]   Craig Valli, Andrew Woodward, The 2008 Australian Study of Remnant Data Contained on 2nd Hand Hard Disks: The Saga Continues, The 6th Australian Digital Forensics Conference, Perth, Western Australia, December 1-3, 2008, <URL: http://conferences.secau.org/proceedings/2008/forensics/Valli%20and%20Woodward%202008%20remnant%20Data%20saga%20continues.pdf>.

[Vaq09]   Luis M. Vaquero1, Luis Rodero-Merino1, Juan Caceres, Maik Lindner, A Break in the Clouds: Towards a Cloud Definition, Computer Communication Review (CCR) Online, Short technical Notes, January 2009, <URL: http://ccr.sigcomm.org/online/files/p50-v39n11-vaqueroA.pdf>.

[Vie09]   Kleber Vieira, Alexandre Schulter, Carlos Westphall, Carla Westphall, Intrusion Detection Techniques in Grid and Cloud Computing Environment, IT Professional, IEEE Computer Society, August 26, 2009.

[Vij11]   Jaikumar Vijayan, City of Los Angeles May Sue over Delays in Google Apps Project, Computer World, April 18, 2011, <URL: http://computerworld.co.nz/news.nsf/management/city-of-los-angeles-may-sue-over-delays-in-google-apps-project-report>.

[Vmw09]   VMware Hosted Products and Patches for ESX and ESXi Resolve a Critical Security Vulnerability, VMware Security Advisory, VMSA-2009-0006, <URL: http://www.vmware.com/security/advisories/VMSA-2009-0006.html>.

[Vmw10]   VMware vShield: Virtualization-Aware Security for the Cloud, product brochure, 2010, <URL: http://www.vmware.com/files/pdf/vmware-vshield_br-en.pdf>.

[Wai08]   Phil Wainewright. Many Degrees of Multi-tenancy, ZDNET News and Blogs, June 16, 2008, <URL: http://blogs.zdnet.com/SAAS/?p=533>.

[Wal10]   Hannah Wald, Cloud Computing for the Federal Community, IAnewsletter, Vol. 13, No. 2, Information Assurance Technology Analysis Center, Spring 2010.

[Wei09]   Jinpeng Wei, Xiaolan Zhang, Glenn Ammons, Vasanth Bala, Peng Ning, Managing Security of Virtual Machine Images in a Cloud Environment, ACM Cloud Computing Security Workshop (CCSW'09) , Chicago, Illinois, November 13, 2009.

[Wei11]   Thilo Weichert, Cloud Computing and Data Privacy, The Sedona Conference, Working Group on International Electronic Information Management, Discovery & Disclosure, February 2011, <URL: https://www.datenschutzzentrum.de/cloud-computing/20100617-cloud-computing-and-data-privacy.pdf>.

[Whi09]   Lance Whitney, Amazon EC2 Cloud Service Hit by Botnet, Outage, December 11, 2009, CNET News, <URL: http://news.cnet.com/8301-1009_3-10413951-83.html>.

[Wil10]   Matt Williams, All Eyes are on Los Angeles as City Deploys Cloud-Based E-Mail, Government Technology, February 10, 2010, <URL: http://www.govtech.com/gt/744804?id=744804&full=1&story_pg=1>.

[Xen08]   Xen Architecture Overview, Version 1.2, Xen Wiki Whitepaper, February 13, 2008, <URL: http://wiki.xensource.com/xenwiki/XenArchitecture?action=AttachFile&do=get&target=Xen+Architecture_Q1+2008.pdf>.

[You07]   Greg Young, Neil MacDonald, John Pescatore, Limited Choices are Available for Network Firewalls in Virtualized Servers, Gartner, Inc., ID Number: G00154065, December 20, 2007, <URL: http://www.reflexsystems.com/Content/News/20071220-GartnerVirtualSecurityReport.pdf>.

[You08]   Lamia Youseff, Maria Butrico, Dilma Da Silva, Toward a Unified Ontology of Cloud Computing, Grid Computing Environments Workshop (GCE08), held in conjunction with SC08, November 2008, <URL: http://www.cs.ucsb.edu/~lyouseff/CCOntology/CloudOntology.pdf>.

[Zet09a]   Kim Zetter, FBI Defends Disruptive Raids on Texas Data Centers, Wired Magazine, April 7, 2009, <URL: http://www.wired.com/threatlevel/2009/04/data-centers-ra/>.

[Zet09b]   Kim Zetter, Bank Sends Sensitive E-mail to Wrong Gmail Address, Sues Google, Wired Magazine, September 21, 2009, <URL: http://www.wired.com/threatlevel/2009/09/bank-sues-google/>.

Appendix A—Acronyms

CAPTCHA	Completely Automated Public Turing test to tell Computers and Humans Apart
CRM	Customer Relationship Management
ESI	Electronically Stored Information
FISMA	Federal Information Security Management Act
FOIA	Freedom of Information Act
FTP	File Transfer Protocol
HIPAA	Health Insurance Portability and Accountability Act
HVAC	Heating, Ventilation, and Air Conditioning
IA	Information Assurance
IaaS	Infrastructure as a Service
MX	Mail eXchange
NARA	National Archives and Records Administration
NAT	Network Address Translation
OECD	Organization for Economic Co-operation and Development
OMB	Office of Management and Budget
PaaS	Platform as a Service
PCI DSS	Payment Card Industry Data Security Standard
PDP	Policy Decision Point
PEP	Policy Enforcement Point
PIA	Privacy Impact Assessment
PII	Personally Identifiable Information
SaaS	Software as a Service
SSAE	Standards for Attestation Engagements
SORN	System of Records Notice
SECS	SaaS E-mail and Collaboration Solution
SAML	Security Assertion Markup Language
SLA	Service Level Agreement
SOAP	Simple Object Access Protocol (originally)
SPI	Sensitive Personal Information
US-CERT	United States Computer Emergency Readiness Team
WPA	WiFi Protected Access
XACML	eXtensible Access Control Markup Language
XML	eXtensible Markup Language

Appendix B—Online Resources

The table below contains a list of online resources that may be helpful to security professionals and other readers of this publication in gaining a greater understanding of cloud computing security and privacy issues and possible mitigations.

Resource Description	URL
DRAFT Cloud Computing Synopsis and Recommendations, NIST, May 2011	http://csrc.nist.gov/publications/drafts/800-146/Draft-NIST-SP800-146.pdf
Challenging Security Requirements for US Government Cloud Computing Adoption (Draft), Cloud Security Working Group, NIST, November 2011	http://collaborate.nist.gov/twiki-cloud-computing/pub/CloudComputing/CloudSecurity/NIST_Security_Requirements_for_US_Government_Cloud.pdf
Top Threats to Cloud Computing, V1.0, Cloud Security Alliance, March 2010	http://www.cloudsecurityalliance.org/topthreats/csathreats.v1.0.pdf
Privacy Recommendations for the Use of Cloud Computing by Federal Departments and Agencies, CIO Council, Privacy Committee, August 19,2010	http://www.cio.gov/documents/Privacy-Recommendations-Cloud-Computing-8-19-2010.docx
Security Guidance For Critical Areas of Focus in Cloud Computing, V2.1, Cloud Security Alliance, December 2009	http://www.cloudsecurityalliance.org/csaguide.pdf
Cloud Computing Risk Assessment, European Network and Information Security Agency, November 2009	http://www.enisa.europa.eu/act/rm/files/deliverables/cloud-computing-risk-assessment/at_download/fullReport
The 10 Worst Cloud Outages (and what we can learn from them), J R Raphael, InfoWorld, June 27, 2011	http://www.infoworld.com/d/cloud-computing/the-10-worst-cloud-outages-and-what-we-can-learn-them-902
The Future of Cloud Computing, Version 1.0, Commission of the European Communities, Expert Group on Cloud Computing, January 2010	http://cordis.europa.eu/fp7/ict/ssai/docs/cloud-report-final.pdf

www.ingramcontent.com/pod-product-compliance
Lightning Source LLC
Chambersburg PA
CBHW060458060326
40689CB00020B/4567